# TILLAMOOK LIGHT

Tillamook Rock Light-house (as seen from the northwestward).  Fog-siren.

Tillamook Head.

Tillamook  Head.

Tillamook Rock Light-house (as seen from the westward).

Farther land in clouds.          Tillamook Rock Light-house, SE., 6 miles.

Ne-ah-kah-nie Mountain, 1,600 feet.          Cape Falcon.
Tillamook Rock Light-house, SE. by S., 7 miles.

Sketches from the 1889 *Pacific Coast Pilot*, showing Tillamook Rock Light Station as seen from the ocean. Note the great overhang at the west end, in the upper left illustration. That massive hunk of basalt was sheered off in later years by crashing seas.

*Other Books by James A. Gibbs*
*Published by Binford & Mort*


PACIFIC GRAVEYARD
SHIPWRECKS OF THE PACIFIC COAST
SENTINELS OF THE NORTH PACIFIC
SHIPWRECKS OFF JUAN DE FUCA

# TILLAMOOK LIGHT

A *true narrative* of Oregon's
*Tillamook Rock Lighthouse*

James A. Gibbs

**Binford & Mort Publishing**
Portland, Oregon

# DEDICATION

*To the memory of my mother*
*who put up with a maverick son*

# ACKNOWLEDGMENT

To Sam Foster, "Mr. Good Guy" of Seaside, Oregon, who more than any other has kept the spirit of Tillamook Rock alive. His unique Seaside Photo Shop, his news and TV coverage (KGW TV 8, Portland) have kept the public well informed on the latter-day occurrences involving not only the rock but also other segments of the colorful Oregon coast. Several of his excellent photos (including the cover picture) are featured.

*Tillamook Light*
Copyright © 1979 by Binford & Mort Publishing

Printed in the United States of America
Library of Congress Catalog Card Number: 79-65015
ISBN: 0-8323-0334-8

First Edition 1979
Second Printing 1995

# FOREWORD

For a century, lonely Tillamook Rock and its lighthouse have
been a sentimental part of Oregon. A warning beacon to thousands of vessels skirting the coast or bound for the Columbia
River bar, it was known to mariners the world over, and adopted
by the resort towns of Seaside and Cannon Beach. Standing ever
vigilant, manned by faithful attendants, it warned ships away
from the surrounding marine graveyard for eight decades. Then
in 1957, its light went out forever.

One of America's three most famous—and at the same time
infamous—wave-swept offshore lighthouses, Tillamook Light
was, on completion in 1881, considered a great engineering triumph, but a structure that was to take an unmerciful beating
from the elements in the years that followed.

*Tillamook Light* tells its colorful story, from oil lamps to electricity, from important navigational aid to dilapidation. This is
an authentic personal account using actual names and situations.
The first *Tillamook Light* was published in 1953, but because
the main characters were still living, the text was fictionalized.

The aids to navigation mission of the U.S. Coast Guard has a
history dating back to the building and illumination of the first
American lighthouse on Little Brewster Island in Boston Harbor
in 1716. At first, because of the indifference of England, local
or Colonial governments had to shoulder the responsibility of
making the waters safe for mariners. Following independence,
the newly created Congress of the United States formed the
Lighthouse Establishment as an administrative unit of the Federal Government, on August 7, 1789. Before being transferred to
and consolidated with the U.S. Coast Guard, July 1, 1939, it was
under the Lighthouse Board or the U.S. Lighthouse Service and
later the Bureau of Lighthouses, from 1852 to 1939. During the
active years of Tillamook Rock Light Station, the lighthouse
served under the latter branches.

Tillamook Rock Light stands as a symbol of man's relentless
fight against the cruelties of the sea. The monolith on which it

stands still resists the buffetings of the Pacific as it has for countless centuries. Great seas still break over it and the winds continue their assault with unabated fury.

No story of a lighthouse would be complete without relating the problems and heartbreaking difficulties that beset the builders, or those who manned the station, particularly at such a harsh location. It has been a battle of men against the sea, epics of daring and endurance—and an ever-present touch of humor.

The most magnificent of lighthouses was perhaps built some 2,200 years ago, the lofty Pharos of Alexandria, near the mouth of the Nile, but to this writer that classification belonged to Tillamook Rock Lighthouse during its active years.

From its inception, Tillamook Light had defied all dire predictions of its impending disaster. Originally labeled as the "hoodoo light," in many minds it was but a matter of time until it would be tumbled into the sea, as was the first lighthouse on Minot's Ledge. Gloomy prophets predicted that no human beings would be willing or able to endure the hardships of such a station. Yet, men were found who did endure the peculiarities, the dangers, the privation and the loneliness. The light kept shining and the foghorn blasting until the day Uncle Sam decided that the antique sentinel was no longer essential to safe navigation.

No one can say how many ships from the nations of the world were guided by Tillamook Rock's faithful beams of light during its heyday, but it was one of many navigational signposts marking America's principal searoads. Ever since man took to the ocean to earn his daily bread, he has depended on lights along the shore. For centuries he sailed the seven seas when lights were few. He steered his fragile ships, guided by omens, superstitions and some knowledge of astronomy. Later came the cross staff and the astrolabe, crude instruments that enabled him to get an angle on the sun to estimate his approximate position. Next came the quadrant, sextant, compass and the chronometer.

As knowledge of navigation increased, there were crude "logs" to measure a vessel's speed. Then, through the use of mathematics and more advanced astronomy, celestial navigation came into its own. A fantastic breakthrough occurred in the early 1920's when radio was introduced to navigators. In sequence, radar, sonar, radio beacons and Loran revolutionized navigation, and with the advent of automation and computerization, the traditional old lighthouse that had held sway from the time man first hoisted a sail, became a secondary necessity to men of the sea.

Though the keepers are gone and many lighthouses retired, lights and horns still function, and the fear of the dangerous outcrops along the shore still remains. From the earliest seafarers down to the masters of the mammoth supertankers of our day, one common fear remains—oddly enough, the fear of land. In the windship era, many rough, tough skippers, totally relaxed at sea, became nervous tyrants when faced with the obsession of coastal shipwreck. Some skippers are known to have locked themselves in their cabins on making a landfall, and, even today, almost every shipmaster will confess to a certain apprehension on nearing land after crossing an ocean.

The so-called "blue-water men" in olden times always downgraded the coastwise navigators, especially along the Pacific coast. Actually it was the latter who not only faced the greatest danger but were often the best at their trade. Constantly they dodged other ships in the heavily traveled steamer lanes, hopped from one doghole to the next, darted in and out of tight bar entrances, and battled pea-soup fogs and white-maned seas, which were often pockmarked with reefs and rocks waiting to tear apart any vessel unfortunate enough to get a mile off course.

It is little wonder that coast mariners had a much greater appreciation of lights along the shore—the least of which was Tillamook Light. As for the landlubbers of Oregon, the rock was a part of them too. Nearly all of the material used in the construction of the lighthouse came from Oregon sources. Hard black Clackamas stone, 8,500 cubic feet of it, was barged to Astoria and loaded aboard the U.S. revenue cutter *Thomas Corwin* for transportation to the rock. The 96,600 bricks used in the project are also believed to have been kilned somewhere in the state. Katherine O'Neill, of Portland, recalls that her grandfather supplied the iron and steel. The building of the lighthouse—under the direction of Col. G.L. Gillespie, army engineer who was also on the Lighthouse Service Board—was ranked in Washington, D.C. headquarters as a "notable achievement." Colonel Gillespie later became Chief of Army Engineers.

# CONTENTS

Appendix I

Observations of the eminent George Davidson, U.S. Coast and Geodetic Survey, concerning Tillamook Rock and its lighthouse.

Appendix II

Federal political climate during the tenure of duty of Tillamook Rock Light Station, 1881-1957.

Appendix III

Principal Keepers of Tillamook Rock Lighthouse.

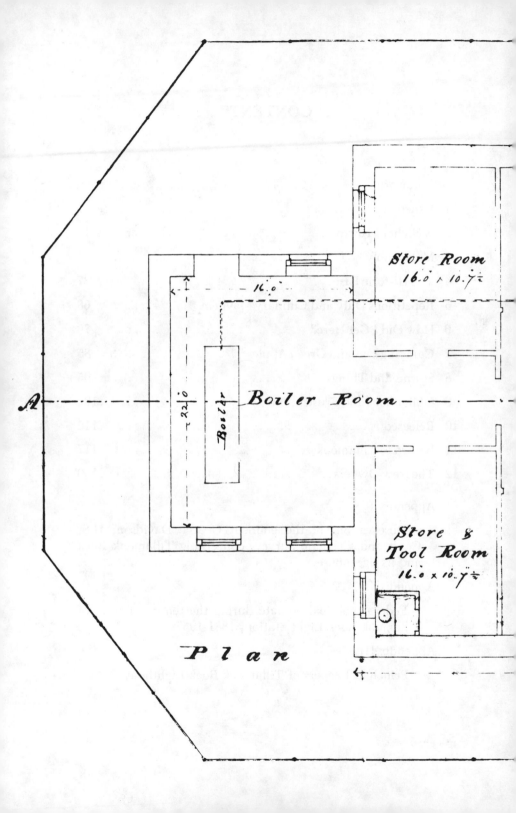

Store Room
16.0 × 10.7½

Boiler Room

Boiler

11.0

22.0

A

Store &
Tool Room
16.0 × 10.7½

Plan

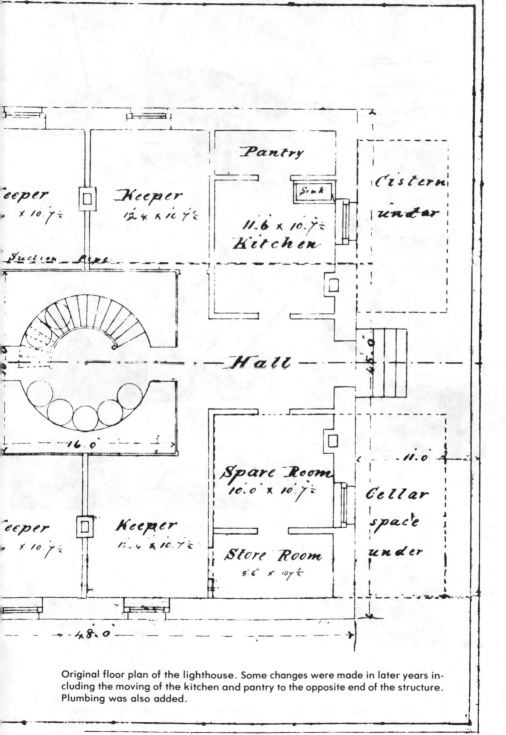

Original floor plan of the lighthouse. Some changes were made in later years including the moving of the kitchen and pantry to the opposite end of the structure. Plumbing was also added.

GLENMORAG 1896

POTRIMPOS 1896

GLENMORAG 1896

PETER IREDALE 1906

SOLANO 1907

LUPATIA 1881

PETER IREDALE 1906

The purpose of Tillamook Light was to warn ships away from the jaws of destruction, especially from the graveyard of ships at the entrance of the Columbia River. Pictured here are some of the ill-fated vessels that came to grief.

# CHAPTER 1

# EXILED

The lighthouse keeper has gone the way of the iceman and the blacksmith, but his story remains. Here are the unique adventures I experienced as a lighthouse keeper on a seagirt piece of real estate off Oregon's timeless shores. Since that adventure at Tillamook Rock lighthouse, more than a couple of decades have passed, during which automation, computerization and many other remarkable innovations, such as television, have become an accepted way of life.

Since my experiences, the main characters have all passed on and the infamous "Terrible Tilly" was long ago bugled out of active service. Reduced from riches to rags since its retirement in 1957, the decaying structure has gone through three private owners, each of which fought a futile battle to preserve what has become a white elephant. The rock defies all efforts at revival, due in great part to its geographical inaccessibility.

Through binding decree, the Coast Guard in 1957 declared that the rusting lantern room should never again display a light in its crown. As the elements go about their inevitable work of destruction, legions of seabirds zero in on the timeless crag, claiming it as their rookery and general-purpose air terminal, whitening the precipitous rock with their droppings.

But let us go back to the hectic days of 1945 when World War II was winding down. I remember one winter morning well— cold, sullen, the wind blasts cutting like a whetted knife. The engine purred as the 52-foot motor lifeboat pitched and rolled her way toward the Columbia River bar. Gripping the railing, I looked at the ominous clouds hanging precariously like the top of a huge circus tent, painting the heaving sea an eerie gray. Toward the horizon it was as if a deep, black ditch dropped off into nothingness. The wind gusts nipped off the crests of the mountainous swells, blowing the spume into a lather of spray.

Astern, beyond our erratic wake, shoalwaters stretched endlessly away to the north and south. Lost in the murky distance were the Coast Guard station behind Point Adams and the skylines of Astoria and Ilwaco. As the seas increased in intensity, the shuddering craft responded to the thrust of the screw, nosing over a titanic roller abreast the jetty, dropping in a trough, and then climbing to the peak of another roller.

In my stomach, a total of two fried eggs rested uneasily. The grizzled helmsman glanced at me periodically, seeming to enjoy the green glow at my gills. He laughed as he told me the worst was yet to come. A distorted smile came over my face, and a burning sensation gripped my interior.

My jovial shipmate was joined shortly by the bo's'n, who emerged from the hatch gnawing on a piece of greasy meat. After a few casual remarks he turned toward me.

"Tillamook Rock," he muttered, "I wouldn't take that duty on a bet."

My attention was diverted. I was more concerned at the moment about keeping the eggs down than pondering his trite remark.

"You can have the rock," he persisted, "I don't want any part of it."

"That makes two of us," remarked his cohort.

I tried to pretend I wasn't much interested, but my ears automatically stood at attention for I knew virtually nothing of the place except that vacancies were reserved for troublemakers.

"Remember the time we took the guy off the rock in a straight jacket?" said the bo's'n to the other.

"Yah! He was a real section eight."

By then, the lifeboat was taking it green over the bow and I renewed my hold on the nearest stanchion. Our sou'westers were matted with salt, our rubber boots sloshing in six inches of bilge

A quiet Sunday at the rock in the early 1940s.

Precipitous wall of basalt. The derrick boom is seen hovering over the Pacific, which is in one of its calmer moods.

water. The boat shook herself like a wet poodle as she rounded the buoy off the jetty and pursued a southerly course. Jostled about by the rushing pyramids of water, she flung herself at the opposition like a football guard.

After a few hours of rigorous voyaging in that seagoing elevator, the bo's'n yelled in my ear.

"See that speck? That's where you're going, mate."

He handed me the glasses. I peered at the watery crests of hissing, yeasty foam. My stomach felt empty at what I saw, but probably more so because those two eggs were no longer there.

Suddenly the haze parted as if Mother Nature had waved it away. The speck grew ever larger and more ominous as the lifeboat neared. Savage breakers lashed its sides—blockbusters that had traveled miles across the Pacific only to snub their noses and explode in an awesome display of lacey spray. The chilling wind stung my inquisitive eyes as I glanced at the sea, at the sky and then back at the rock. The ocean was enormous. Obvious consternation wrinkled the faces of the lifeboat crew, though all four had probably made the run to the rock many times before.

"Better wake up!" the helmsman yelled to another of the crew sacked out below. "May be rough sledding."

The sleeping individual, doubling as cook and machinist's mate in the absence of the former, was catching some winks. His immunity to the pitch and roll was nothing short of amazing.

As the craft jockeyed closer, the dank odor of seaweed and bird droppings filled my nostrils. The bastion-like walls that rose before us were almost frightening. Seemingly casting an evil shadow over us, the ocean lifted the boat to a pinnacle and then dropped it into a bottomless pit. Barnacles and mussels, huge ones, were exposed, thick and slimy around the girth of the rock like the fouled boot topping of a monstrous merchant ship.

We had traveled some 20 miles south from the mouth of the Columbia River, and here out in the ocean, completely exposed to the elements more than a mile offshore, was Tillamook Rock, one of the most unusual basaltic masses I had ever beheld. The rock at best covered less than a quarter acre at its plateau and it was filled almost entirely by the lighthouse. No place was there any

vegetation. I felt I was indeed "between a rock and a hard place."
The giant stone building stood nearly a 100 feet above sea level,
its tower, I was informed, reaching 134 feet into the lowering sky,
surrounded by that ever-penetrating odor one might associate
with a marine graveyard.

I couldn't really believe that I was going to be a resident of such
an isolated place; it seemed more like a pint-sized Alcatraz and
that I was about to serve my sentence as an undesirable service
man. And, admittedly, that was the reason for my new assignment. I had already been informed that those who manned this
stationary ship were old-time career civil-service employees, the
last of the U.S. Lighthouse Service personnel, permitted to remain in their former status when the Coast Guard took over that
branch of the Commerce Department in 1939. Those doughty
individuals, as I was later to find out, were better suited to such
isolated duty for long periods than were the younger Coast
Guardsmen like myself.

The sight before me was unlike any I had ever seen. I wondered
how anyone could get onto the rock with the rise and fall of the
sea being not less than ten feet. The wind was nearly 30 knots and
the water rough and surging, hardly the most desirable situation
for a landing. I had all I could do just to hang tight to what
seemed a runaway bronc from a rodeo.

The boat crew appeared to know what they were doing, but it
seemed to me that one wrong move could mean a one-way ticket
to Davy Jones's Locker. Our lifeboat was like a match stick below
that monolith of wave-lashed basalt, an encumbrance that had
probably been shouldering a losing battle against the ocean since
Noah rode the ark.

Atop the sheer walls stood three individuals peering down at us
like vultures, totally absorbed in the gyrating movements of our
craft which was turning in slow circles. In a small building
perched on the eastern slope of the rock another man, faintly visible, worked the hoist controls. Suddenly, over the sounds of the
wind and surging surf there was a grinding noise and a huge
wooden boom began swinging slowly like the neck of a cautious
giraffe. It halted its arc above our restless craft. A swaying cable

began threading downward toward the water as our craft pitched and rolled violently, holding cautiously to the 50-foot distance from the sinister base of the bastion. When in the right position, the boat's engine began idling but the ocean's motion would not cooperate. Directed toward the fo'c'sle, it was all I could do to make my way forward.

"Here!" shouted the bo's'n, tapping me on the shoulder, "this is for you!"

He handed me a life ring with a pair of oversized canvas pants protruding from a hole in the center.

"Take it" he insisted, "it's a breeches buoy."

"What in blazes do I do with it?" I retorted.

"You want to get up on the rock, don't you?"

I nodded my head feebly.

"Then jump into the pants and hop up on the fo'c'sle head and wait till we get under the cable hook."

Like a drunken sailor, I struggled to position, trying to keep my equilibrium with one hand and hold up my newly acquired "bloomers" with the other. With rubbery legs I finally stood erect. From my position, the top of the lighthouse seemed to touch the low-hanging clouds, but what occupied my mind was how I could hold the breeches buoy with one hand and at the same time hook the ring on the attached ropes into the cable hook.

The boat moved slowly once again until we were directly under the swinging cable.

"Hook it! Hook it!" hollered the bo's'n.

As I reached skyward, he turned his attention to the man at the wheel.

"Look sharp! Look sharp there, or she'll be into that whirlpool. Ease off!"

The boat heeled ungraciously and rose again on a huge swell, gathering speed while every bolt seemingly wrenched in its socket.

I stood on tiptoe and grabbed for the hook. Just then the craft took a decided lurch and I went sprawling, grabbing the nearest solid thing to keep from going overboard. I could hear oaths of profanity as the boat shuddered, water pouring over the fantail.

Up, up and away. Coastguardsman lifted from the deck of the motor lifeboat for transit to the rock.

Nothing quite compared with the aerial ride to and from the station landing platform.

For a moment we steadied on a ridge of liquid. Too busy maneuvering the bucking craft to be concerned about me, the crew displayed their seamanship abilities in getting us back into position.

Securing the breeches buoy around my waist once again, I spread my feet apart, braced myself and waited. Again the boat came up under the cable hook.

"Grab the damn thing! Grab it!" a voice shouted at me.

This time I connected with the eyebolt, but before catching my breath, my feet went out from under me and I was dragged unceremoniously over the fo'c'sle head, ensconced in the breeches buoy. As the bo's'n signaled to the figure in the derrick house, I felt the ropes of the conveyance tighten. Over the side I went, floundering in the coldest water this side of solid ice. I thought my death warrant had been signed, when with a terrific jerk I ascended from the depths like a hooked fish—up, up, dangling some 75 feet above the swirling waters boiling against the defiant precipice below. For a moment I thought I had sprouted wings, but quickly realized that once yanked from the brine, my survival was now dependent on the flimsy contraption that held me between sea and sky.

The lifeboat dwindled in size below me. Strong gusts hampered the turning of the boom for what seemed an eternity as I sat there rocking, the chill wind making ice sheets of my wet clothing. When the machine in the derrick house finally mustered enough power to swing the boom, I breathed a bit easier but kept wondering why amusement park promoters had never given this invention a whirl.

When the boom finally terminated its arc, I was directly over a slab of concrete set in the black, basaltic mass. As the cable payed out, the scene below flashed dismally. At the plateau of the rock the huge, square stone building, crowned by a tower, loomed ever larger. The east slope of the rock, where I was to land, slid into the ocean like the laced portion of an old man's shoe. The southern exposure was broken by a deep fissure where the breakers roared in and shot geysers of spray skyward. Dropping vertically into the sea were the precipitous north and western slopes, the latter with a definite overhang. A feeling of futility came over me, the like of which I had never before experienced. At the moment I would have given a king's ransom for a return ticket to the mainland.

As the platform came up to meet me, a pair of weathered hands reached upward and guided me to solid ground. I was joined by yet another who stood dressed in civilian clothes, a small suitcase at his side. As I struggled out of the breeches buoy, the slightly graying man with the suitcase scrambled into the conveyance. It was obvious he was eager and anxious for his shore leave. Before any words were exchanged, I watched the breeches buoy become airborne once again, then stood alone with the one who had guided me down.

"George is the name," he volunteered, "George Wheeler. Yah better get topside and get them wet duds off. Ask for Allik, he'll show you where to go."

I noted the suitcase still stood on the platform, plus a big canvas sack full of letters and packages waiting to be off-loaded. My seabag was still aboard the lifeboat but, instead of waiting, I heeded the advice of the keeper on the landing platform and went topside, shivering as if icicles were down my back.

I left George behind—a relatively tall, large-boned individual, slightly lanky and on the 60 side of life—and started up the cement stairway that had been poured into the rock. On my way, I passed the derrick house and got a better look at the man at the controls. Slight and wiry with whitish hair, he gave me a half wave while concentrating on the levers. I wanted to ask him why he dragged me through the brine, but the time wasn't right. I looked down into the watery chasm in time to see the vacationing keeper being dropped to the boat. For a time he wavered in the air and I wondered if he too would get a dunking. Fortune was with him, however, two crewmen aiding him while the man at the wheel managed to hold the boat steady.

Just as I reached the entrance to the lighthouse, I turned back once again to see a cargo net being attached to the cable hook, with supplies, mail and my seabag contained therein.

I was impressed with the exterior of the lighthouse, solid stone blocks better than two feet thick, fit together with precision.

Above the curved archway of the entrance, cut deep into the stone, were the following words:

TILLAMOOK ROCK L.H.

ERECTED 1880

LON. 124° 01′ W.

LAT. 45° 56′ N.

It appeared that the white, painted edifice had stood well the test of time, though it was obvious everywhere I looked that Mother Nature's anger had left numerous jagged scars.

The author at entrance of Tillamook Rock Lighthouse.

Still dripping as if out of a shower, a trail of water marked my footsteps on entering the building. A short entrance through a storm door left me standing in a spacious hallway or foyer. At the center was an iron circular staircase that wound ever upward into the tower, while bordering the hall was a series of bedrooms. I continued through the building, the thickness of the walls shutting out the sounds of the wind and sea. It felt strange to stand there alone, not hearing any human stirrings. Shortly after passing a storeroom I heard the clatter of pans and silverware and then found myself in the kitchen face to face with a third keeper, whom I assumed to be Allik. I introduced myself and told him about my dunking.

"Happens often, especially when it's rough," he said with a slight accent.

Allik was a shy, soft-spoken individual, but friendly. Estonian by birth, he said he had come over from the old Country while a young man, immediately applying for and later being accepted into government service. His first assignment duty had been aboard the Columbia River Lightship. He informed me that George was the head keeper, or as they said in Lighthouse Service language, the principal keeper.

Allik, whose first name was Oswald (Ozzie), showed me to my room at the east end of the building, but did not come in.

"One rule we keep here," he said, "is we stay out of each other's bedroom. Gets pretty lonesome with no place to go and we got to respect each other's privacy."

With that, he left me at the door. I went inside the 10x10-foot room, which contained a bed and an old dresser with a linoleum of sorts on the floor. An ocean view was afforded through a single ship's porthole offering a southerly exposure. It was apparent that a window had once been where the porthole was fitted, for I was soon to learn that the fury of the southerly gales had taken its toll, repeatedly having shattered storm panes and window frames. The rugged porthole, set deep in the stone, contained inch-thick glass. Even then, I could see numerous nicks where debris had been flung against it.

As I looked around my cell, many thoughts passed through my mind and most were negative. The trance was broken with a knock at my door, but on opening it, nobody was there. Instead, my seabag was standing at attention. I was quick to get off my wet clothes.

Everywhere I looked, the place took on more of the aspects of an insane asylum instead of what I had pictured a lighthouse to be. I wondered if they would give me a Section Eight—psychologically unfit—before completing the first hitch of my sentence. It was all I could do to keep from running back to the landing platform and pleading to be removed. In fact, I did go to the entrance again, looking out in agony as the motor lifeboat corkscrewed away from the rock, plowing into heavy seas. For the first time it struck me solidly that I would be here for three long months before the coveted time off. For one who was used to people and places, this would be a challenge. It was as if I had been exiled forever from civilization.

When night came on dark and eerie, I could see the hint of lights at the distant resorts of Seaside and Cannon Beach. I knew for the first time what men imprisoned at Alcatraz, in the center of San Francisco Bay, must have felt. Here alone was I with three career lighthouse keepers all considerably older than myself, none of whom appeared too happy to have a young Coast Guardsman added to their ranks—a replacement for another who had failed to endure the loneliness and privation.

After I had collected my thoughts, and before being schooled in my assignments, my tour of the lighthouse continued. The structure was 64x45 feet, slightly indented at the western extremity, which consisted of a 16x22-foot fog signal room where the generators and compressors for the fog sirens were located. A coal bin and oil-storage tanks were also there, plus a half-filled punching bag hanging from the ceiling. A concrete walk about 12 feet wide rimmed the entire structure, with little room left for anything else at the plateau of the rock. Huge metal fuel and water tanks were located outside the structure at the eastern and western ends, and I couldn't help noticing the rust streaks from the salt air that had attacked everything made of metal, including the railing.

The rear door was at the northwesterly section of the building, below which was a straight 90-foot drop to the ocean. The northeast portion contained a small paint and storage locker and tiny but solid, reinforced, masonry privy. Talk about your brick outhouses—this one capped them all. Curiosity led me to inspect and what I saw inside made me shudder. It was a one-holer, the hole dropping directly to the ocean, and the wind vacuum coming up through it was like a small tornado. I got to thinking that sitting on that wind tunnel could greatly hamper nature's calling. I worried about that until I went back into the fog signal room and discovered that there was a bathroom, be it ever so small, with a toilet and a vintage bathtub. Later I was told of the great rejoicing when plumbing finally came to the rock. The privy over the precipice had probably caused more than one lighthouse keeper to change his occupation, and later on, I was to learn why.

In the kitchen, or the galley (a personal choice of the individual), I encountered Allik once again and pried him with questions. He had his hands full preparing the evening meal and I assumed he was the regular cook. When informed that each keeper took his turn on a rotation basis, I nearly swallowed my tongue. I couldn't even boil water and make it come out right.

The kitchen was simple—a stove that could cook and heat the room, old wooden cupboards, a plain table and four stiff-backed chairs. A small pantry was attached to the room, and for all intents and purposes this area was the center of the social activities for this stationary rock-bottomed ship. A desk of sorts for lighthouse business and for entries in the lighthouse log was kept in plain sight.

Entered George, the potentate. In rather gruff terms he informed me watches were kept around the clock. The light was turned on an hour before sunset and turned off an hour after sunrise. Whenever the weather thickened and the visibility was less than two miles, the foghorn was activated. Hourly inspections were made night and day, and every afternoon except Sunday, the complete routine of lighthouse cleaning was pursued. Maintenance of machinery was a necessity, and exterior painting was done when weather conditions warranted. Most things were in duplicate—foghorns, compressors, generators and electrical systems. A standby kerosene lamp was available for placement in the lens should the electrical systems short out.

Three keepers stood eight-hour watches; the cook did his own thing.

"Yah got the midnight watch," said George, "and," he added, "Yah better not fall asleep."

Without hesitation he proceeded to show me the "ropes," as he called them.

Before returning to my room I made a final inspection of my new home, climbing up the spiral staircase that entered into a watch room. Cold and damp, it had a huge iron storm door that led to an outside gallery. Another small iron staircase took me up to the lantern room where stood a huge eight-eyed areo-marine beacon, which I was to learn later was installed after a howling 1934 southwesterly gale had shattered the glass prisms of the lighthouse's original first-order French-made lens. I could not believe it when told that seas sometimes leaped 134 feet to the top of the lantern, breaking the window panes, the lens prisms and filling the tower's interior with rocks and debris.

There I stood alone surveying this strange hunk of real estate that had defied the block-busting ocean ramparts for untold years. Men had challenged and conquered this conical mass many decades earlier, placing a sentinel atop its crest. As I looked down into the gray gloom of sea and sky, dusk slowly settled in. The ocean hissed and rolled, slashing mercilessly against the base of the rock, and the winds whistled around the circular lantern house in weird crescendos. I felt even lonelier than before; it was like a bad dream that would soon end, but instead, it was only the beginning.

Soon it would be time for the bulging glass-eyed monster to start its slow rotation, sending 80,000 candlepower flashes of light to sea, warning of the dangers of this basaltic obstruction off Oregon's salty coast. It gave one a humanitarian feeling, yet at the moment, my inner feelings were anything but along that line. I was suddenly shocked out of my mood when the powerful roar of the foghorn deafened my ears. The weather had closed in and the guttural sound permeated the entire structure.

What had I gotten myself into?

The underside of the spiral staircase in the tower at Tillamook looks much like a conch shell. The station ghost, with its strange moaning sounds, most often haunted this area.

# CHAPTER 2

# A NIGHT OF HORROR

The first evening meal gave me a chance to get to know my cell mates better. Ill at ease, I entered the kitchen where I found eager eaters ready to sink their choppers into Allik's delicacies. Steaming serving dishes were filled with boiled potatoes, vegetables and some type of meat that I couldn't readily identify.

"Okay," said the cook, "eat up."

George sat down like a sack of walnuts, his joints creaking. Allik was much gentler in his approach. The third keeper, whom I had seen in the derrick house, was Roy Dibb, who proved much more sociable than the others. I was soon to learn that his greatest joy in life was golfing, most of his spare leave being spent at the Astoria Country Club, where he consistently shot in the low eighties or high seventies, despite his ripening age.

George's table manners left a little to be desired, perhaps because his false teeth didn't fit too well. Still, he could really stow it away.

"Pass the bread," he demanded, his mouth opening like a cargo hatch. As Roy pushed the plate his way, two slices were swept off with a single stroke.

Allik watched his culinary efforts pass into oblivion. I was thankful I didn't feel very hungry for I might have had to struggle for my fair share. Even the jello dessert vanished in short order.

As the Tillamook crew slurped down their coffee among belches and teeth picking, the conversation somehow got around to the subject of the lighthouse ghost. On certain nights, strange unexplained noises were heard in the tower, they informed me. I was certain these old foxes were trying to frighten a young man as a sort of lighthouse initiation, but then I had always scoffed at such nonsense.

As I was later to learn, every "genuine" lighthouse boasted of having a ghost, some legitimate, others illegitimate, if such terminology can be used. Keepers often heard unseen, unexplained footsteps, saw materials moved around, oil lamps blown out mysteriously and windows and doors left ajar. For some strange reason, ghosts and ghouls seem to favor the architecture of a lighthouse. The solitude and privation leaves a fertile field for the over-active mind. As for the Tillamook wraith, I would have to draw my own conclusion.

Feeling quite exhausted after dinner, I parted company in anticipation of the midnight watch. Going to my room, I gently closed the door, undogged the porthole and let a strong sea breeze blow fresh air into my stuffy domicile. I took in some deep breaths and proceeded to undress. Turning out the light, I flopped into bed and pulled up the covers. The springs dug into my back through a worn-out mattress and for an hour or so I tossed and turned while thinking over the events of the day. I was thankful the foghorn had ceased blowing, but I could think of nothing else to cheer me at the moment.

Finally I dozed off, but shortly after awakened with a start. I was positive I heard footsteps in the room and instantly sprang up to a 90-degree angle. The nerves in my body tensed. Then I remembered the order about keepers not entering another's room. Momentarily relaxing, I assured myself that it was only the pranks of a freshening wind and a restless sea. When I had nearly convinced myself, there was another step, even closer. The light switch was at the other end of the room, but my body suddenly stiffened. How much did I actually know about these strange lighthouse keepers? Was there really a ghost in the tower?

For some reason I just couldn't move. I pinched myself to be sure it wasn't a nightmare, but this was no dream, it was real. I grew rigid all over again and tried to call out, but the utterances seemed to choke in my throat. After hearing two more steps, I knew that whatever it was, was standing next to my bed. Then came that terrifying moment when something passed near my throat, so close that the breeze fanned my face.

Visions of a knife, of violent pain, and warm blood seized me. In the awful darkness, my body suddenly acted from instinct. Swinging my arms wildly with my every ounce of my strength, I leaped from my bed, pillow in front of my face, and charged my attacker like a Notre Dame fullback. Then something tripped me and I went sprawling across the floor. Slamming into the wall, I struck my head and sank my fingernails into the plaster while trying to regain my feet. I felt around in confused haste for the light switch. My heart was beating like a triphammer and it seemed an eternity before the dim globe came to life.

Turning to face my assailant, I nearly collapsed on seeing what was there. A mammoth goose with a broken wing sat in the middle of the floor. Evidently blinded by the beacon, it had flown through the open porthole and broken its wing en route. Each wing flap had resembled a human footstep, and the most dreaded moment must have occurred when the goose leaped up on the chair beside my bed and flapped its wing next to my throat.

The strenuous ordeal left me rigid. I didn't know whether to laugh, cry or scream. Finally I swooped up the bird, which until that moment had made no vocal sounds. Marching him straight outside to the cadence of his honking, I dropped him with a plunk in a sheltered corner of the lighthouse and made haste back to my warm bed to capitalize on a well-earned sleep.

Never was that phantom goose seen again. For all I know he may have walked off the edge of the rock and ended it all. I will confess, however, that if the goose had not been there when I flipped on the light I would indeed have become a staunch believer in ghosts.

My deep sleep was interrupted rudely with a loud pounding on the door. "Your watch!" said the knocker.

After dressing, I made my way to the kitchen where George waited to be relieved.

"What's a matter with yah?" he questioned. "Yah look like you seen a ghost."

For a moment I thought he was psychic, but then I was too embarrassed to tell him what had happened. Besides, he looked tired and eager for bed. As he got up to leave, he turned with a furrowed brow, gruffly stating, "Half-hour checks on everything."

I nodded, then suddenly found myself alone in the kitchen with four walls staring at me. I looked up at the old Regulator clock on the wall, which slowly ticked away the minutes. When the time came for my first rounds, I went outside into the cold, windy night to check the visibility. The atmosphere had cleared somewhat and a slight drizzle pricked my face. The roar of the sea was intense and all around was a black abyss, except when the probing beams of light from the beacon cut the darkness like a knife. For obvious reasons it was scary outside and I was glad to re-enter the fog signal house.

Continuing my rounds, I headed for the tower and began climbing the spiral staircase to check the light. As I ascended, my shoes clattered against the iron grates. The sounds called back at me, echoing off the tower walls. Just before I reached the watch room, I detected another unrelated noise, strange, haunting. Stopping in my tracks, I stood motionless. There it was again, a whispering moan, like one in pain.

"Oh, not again," thought I to myself. The goose was all I could take for one night. But this was different, and the utterance smacked of something human. Could one of the keepers be trying to frighten me? "Oh, you foolish soul," thought I. These old duffers had better things to do than go around playing ghost. Then I got to thinking of the conversation at the dinner table. Were there really such wraiths, I wondered, or were they only a figment of the imagination. I looked all around trying to figure out the source of those strange sounds but could draw no logical conclusion. Thus I hastily parted company with the unseen apparition, scurried into the watch room and then climbed the ladder to the lamp room.

Great flashes of light caused spectrums of color on the wall as the lens turned silently in its carriage. I didn't dare look directly into the beam, so intense was the light source. The reflectors directed the beams 18 miles to sea. As instructed, I took the stop watch and timed the characteristic—one flash every 5 seconds, 0.8 second flash. As far as I could determine with my neophyte lighthouse knowledge, the lens and its electric motor were in excellent shape, doing accurately the job for which they were designed.

Now at last, for just a brief moment, I felt a slight bit useful. Here I was in the "crown room" of old Tillamook Rock Lighthouse, checking the light that beamed its warnings to vessels at sea. Wiping some specks of dust from the lantern panes, I felt bathed in light rays as the flashes fleeted by like dancing nymphs. It was a kind of warm feeling. Out of curiosity, I stopped the lens carriage and opened a metal door to check on one of two 500-watt globes which seemed to be burning with all its heart. Then I noticed some of the marks on the halfdeck where the former first-order lens and lightning apparatus had been cradled, before the fury of the Pacific did its destruction twelve years earlier. As I was later to learn, the lens had been one of the most beautiful at any Pacific light station—hundreds of handground prisms created by a French manufacturer and mounted in a specially made brass framework. For all the world, when illuminated it had been like a monstrous diamond, glistening and glowing in a myriad of color and lucidity.

An oil lamp was once used inside the old lens, a large glass chimney attached to carry the smoke up to the ball-shaped opening in the lantern-house roof. When the lamp was lighted, it sent its diverse rays into powerful beams by refracting the character of the prisms, each one at a different angle, a formula worked out years earlier by the eminent French scientist, Augustin Fresnel. For decades his discoveries gave the French a premier role as manufacturers of lighthouse lenses and related equipment.

It was a sad day at Tillamook when the original apparatus was removed, replaced by an American-made aero-marine beacon. To the mariner at sea, however, only the characteristic and the intensity of the light mattered, not its history.

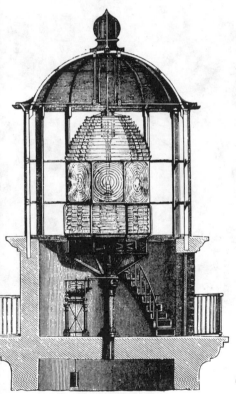

Left: Cutaway sketches of the lantern, lens and lighting apparatus of the First Order of the System of Fresnel, similar to the type used in Tillamook Rock Lighthouse from 1881 till 1935. Right: Scintillating light is reflected through the beautiful first order lens at Tillamook.

Left: Inside a lighthouse lens, a cage of glass and brass, showing a quartz globe as the source of light. Life expectancy of this 1000-watt globe is about 2000 hours. (Harry Gilmore photo) Right: Keeper Ozzie Allik, who put in 20 years on the rock, is pictured standing alongside the aero-marine type beacon placed in the lantern after the first order French-made lens was removed. (Lawrence Barber photo)

I started back down the ladder, satisfied that all was well in the lamp room. Suddenly my thoughts were diverted back to the ghost in the tower. Sure enough, those same sounds were again audible in the same area. I was certain the three keepers were fast asleep at that hour, so it was just the spook and me. Then my eyes fell on a small door near the landing which I had evidently over- looked in surveying the lighthouse. Going back to the kitchen to get a flashlight, I returned to investigate. Could it be that the strange noises were coming from behind that door?

As if playing a role in a mystery movie, I automatically tiptoed toward the entrance. My hand reached for the handle. Timorous, I stepped back as it creaked open. Gathering my self-composure, I bolted inside. The air was dank and there was barely enough headroom to stand erect. As I flashed the light around, shadows played on the wall like hobgoblins around a witch's brew.

Finally I found a light bulb on the ceiling and pulled a pro- truding chain. At first it didn't respond, but finally a dim glow flooded the room which, as I was later to learn, had been created after the original metal lighthouse roof had been holed repeatedly by sea-thrown boulders. It was a storage area of sorts and a place to keep books sent from mainlanders who related to the lonely role of the lighthouse keepers. From the looks of the place nobody ever used it; cobwebs were everywhere. It was like the attic of an early American residence, with a littering of castoffs. What a perfect home for the lighthouse ghost—and certainly a shadowy hideaway that needed future scrutiny. The floor creaked but the moaning sounds I heard in the tower were not in that room.

As the flashlight fell across the sagging bookshelves, I removed two volumes and returned to the more pleasant surroundings of the kitchen.

Making my entry in the log, I sat down to study the literary gems I had taken from the upper room. Blowing a collection of dust from the first, I discovered the auspicious title, *Tom Swift and the Motor Cycle*. Casting it aside, I picked up the other, which told about the old U.S. Lighthouse Service and some of its problems. I thumbed through to an article on the Navassa Light- house on a rock pile in the Caribbean and—wouldn't you know—

on this night of all nights, there was an account of the supernatural. Inasmuch as it was an isolated seagirt lighthouse like
Tillamook, my curiosity was naturally aroused and I read on. It
went something like this:

The head keeper was an individual of 20 years' experience
in lighthouses, quiet, practical and certainly not a believer
in supernatural things. He was chosen to handle the station
after oppressive heat and miserable privation had delayed
its completion till 1917. There was an indescribable something about that small island on the sea road to Panama
(near Haiti and Cuba), rumor persisting that it was cursed,
a holdover from the days when black laborers with white
overlords off-loaded its guano resources. A mutiny among
the workers had created a blood bath in which several were
killed.

That first evening, the keeper-in-charge ascended the
tower staircase (just as I had done *that* very night) and became conscious of the reverberating sound of his feet on the
grates. After tending the light and while returning to the
dwelling for coffee, he was aware of the damp, humid
night, despite a clear, star-laden sky. Then he heard it—a
low, rhythmic wailing sound coming from outside, a sound
resembling a man with a high-pitched voice accompanied
by a shallow drum. Not believing in spooks and such trivia,
despite having served in several lighthouses all claiming
ghosts, he believed in a logical explanation for everything.
Still, curiosity prompted the keeper to open the door and
listen until the whistling wind finally drowned out the
sound.

Nevertheless he took his lantern and inspected the area.
Satisfied that no intruders were about, he started back.
When he reached the dwelling, a loud cackling laugh from
the sea pierced his ears. Believing it a strange combination
of shrieking sea birds, he dismissed it from his mind not
sharing the experience with his assistant.

Two nights passed without consequence. On the third, it happened again. The keeper distinctly heard the same dull throbbing of the drum. While his assistant was winding the weights that turned the lens, he stole silently out into the night. Scurrying toward a clump of wild growth a short distance from the lighthouse, he hid himself from sight. Again the drums began beating, slowly and silently at first, then gaining momentum and volume. The pulsating beat was mingled with the cry of birds and the incessant wind. Then came the same haunting voice that had startled him the first night, this time in a chant. The words sounded like, "Go 'way, white man, go 'way befo' too late!"

It was the call of one troubled, seemingly warning of impending doom. But how could this be? There was nobody else on the island but the two attendants of the lighthouse. He wondered if the oppressive island possessed some strange mysticism. The tempo grew into a wild chant, the apparent warning continuing with greater rapidity as the drums grew ever louder.

While the listener crouched in the thick growth, the chanter's message, in broken English, seemed to be telling of the brutality heaped upon the blacks before the awful Navassa riot of yesteryear. Numbed by it all, the keeper made no attempt to capture his taunter nor was he able to see any clear image. Instead, each night when not on duty, he returned to his secluded listening post to hear the chant. The entire episode smacked of voodoo, and this the keeper knew, but try as he would he could not resist the strange magnetic pull. The keeper became progressively morose and nervous. Alarmed by such behavior, the assistant watched his superior stare for hours on end at the vast sea, tapping his fingers on the table in the same tempo as the voodoo drums. Sometimes he was incoherent, neglecting his duties.

One day, as if in a trance, the troubled man came back to the lighthouse pale as a ghost, chanting a strange jargon and beating his chest in drum-like rhythm. He was stark mad.

By running up distress flags, his frantic associate was able to attract a passing ship. But after signals were exchanged the vessel sailed away and it was two harrowing weeks before a lighthouse tender arrived off the island to remove the demented keeper.

The drums were then suddenly silenced and the voodoo chant was heard no more, nor was its originator, if any, ever found.

For a decade after the incident, the Lighthouse Service maintained personnel at the station, but few could stand the awful privation, the bloodsucking insects and fever. Voodoo rumors persisted all the while.

Finally, in 1929, the Lighthouse Service authorities threw in the sponge, admitting that Navassa was not fit for human habitation. The lighthouse was in turn automated at considerable expense and is still operated with occasional servicing from a buoy tender out of Miami.

It was almost ironic that I should come across such an article on my first night as a lighthouse keeper. I was careful, thereafter, not to take the ghost of Tillamook lightly.

It was one of the longest nights of my life, but finally out of the east a pale glow appeared over towering Tillamook Head, a giant monolith rising from the mainland beach a mile or so east of the rock. A sea mist hung low and the ocean had calmed somewhat. Through the night I had imagined all kinds of things in the shadows and none of them seemed pleasant—clammy, wet, miserable things—the kind that make one wish for desert sunshine. In the days that followed, strange and ghostly visitations were seriously discussed and often considered as omens to be heeded. For some reason, lighthouses seem to spawn more than their share of ghostly tales and supernatural happenings.

My entry in the lighthouse log that morning was routine, for who would have believed my experiences of that night?

# CHAPTER 3

# MELANCHOLY FOG

When wet, gray layers of fog envelope the Oregon Coast, it is almost as if one is blindfolded. Shipmasters and lighthouse keepers become tense. Danger stalks the sea. To live through long sieges of fog is a form of torment, diaphones or air sirens blasting shattering notes at intervals accurate to a split second. So great is the volume of sound and so penetrating, the noise and vibration can become an instrument of torture.

Fog had draped its mantle over the lighthouse for almost a week and the infernal siren had not ceased blowing in all that time—a 5-second blast every 45 seconds, around the clock. It was obvious that such long periods of melancholy had an effect on the lighthouse attendants. We became more easily irritated; there were more arguments and less conversation.

I had been apprised of the fundamental functions of our first-class compressed air siren. It was by no means a modern fixture, having through the years put in thousands of hours of service, blasting its warning through two giant metal trumpets atop the fog-signal building.

According to an old 1896 *Light List* in the files, Tillamook's first fog signal was a steam siren with twin whistles similar to those found on an ocean liner, but it took more than an hour to build up a proper head of steam in the boilers. The air siren, on the other hand, could be put to work immediately by activating the compressors.

Several weeks had passed, and though I had become more accustomed to isolated lighthouse living, those foggy periods were the acid test. I must confess I had given some thought to how one

27

might escape from the rock either by improvised raft or by faking an illness. The former seemed totally foolhardy and the latter would have hurt my pride. Besides, I was a poor liar. Still, living with three others on this tiny piece of terra firma could sometimes be a problem because there were so few places one could be alone. Though always having been around people, in one sense I was a loner and liked having the option of secret places when I so desired. When the storms hit, there was danger outside the lighthouse from boarding seas and flying debris, restricting any outside activities.

Further, there were no radios available, our only communication with the shore being a telephone which was only to be used for service calls and emergencies. Then too, in gales the cable from the mainland sometimes parted. I had not come prepared for the long, lonely hours and thus it was that I found refuge in that strange room with the low ceiling near the tower landing, which I first had thought housed the ghost.

Inasmuch as my cohorts avoided its stuffy climes, I found it a place to cogitate, daydream, pray, read—and play an old wind-up phonograph with some vintage records. Two of my favorites were *No Letter Today* and *Born to Lose*, not exactly barnburners for lessening melancholy, but melodious just the same. I must have played them over a thousand times. My inner sanctum, as I called that room, had a colorful assortment of junk and reading material.

One keeper seldom affected by the fog and inclement weather was Roy. His prowess as a golfer stemmed from a lifetime membership in the "Tillamook Rock Golf and Country Club." The links had no fairways, no greens, no caddies. In fact, he was the only member, but an entirely dedicated one. Fair weather or foul, whenever off duty, his golf ball, tethered with a rope, was attached to a railing stanchion and he swung at that target with the agility of one half his age. During the following weeks I was to see him out there in 40- and 50-mile winds on the lee side of the lighthouse smacking the ball with concentrated gusto. Only when the seas began breaking over the walkway would he grab his driver and ball and head for the "clubhouse." Then he would putt on a small rug in his bedroom.

One day I asked him, "Don't you ever get tired of hitting that thing?"

"It's a real good feelin'," he answered, "when you get just the right clout between the club and the ball."

"It all sounds the same to me," said I.

"That's 'cause your ear isn't attuned," he mused. "It's sort of a psychic thing and a victory of sorts to master that ball."

I couldn't argue with Roy because he had the trophies and the honors that told of his years of success on the mainland links. He openly credited his success to the "Tillamook Rock Country Club" where he found few distractions except occasionally from the weather. A good part of Roy's life had been spent in government service but he had always worked out a proper balance for rest and recuperation when ashore.

He let me have a try at the ball. Taking the club, I whacked at it furiously. Airborne for a moment it wound itself around the stanchion.

Roy shook his head. "Never," he said.

"What do you mean?"

"That would have been a terrible slice."

"How can you be so sure?"

"The clout didn't register. Only a trained ear could tell."

I tried some more shots, but each time got a negative response —slices, hooks, topping the ball, etc.

"You've got a long way to go," Roy said.

Satisfied that I had flunked the golf test, I left the old pro and continued my morning stroll around the lighthouse promenade. The fog filtered in with clammy fingers and as I passed the area where the trumpets were blaring, the noise was ear-shattering. Such a sonorous sound should certainly keep any vessel well away from this obstruction, I kept thinking to myself.

I met Allik coming around the other way, his jacket pulled up tight around his neck. Though his first name was Oswald, for some strange reason his wife Alice called him by his last name and most of his friends had followed suit. His shy tendencies, gentle man that he was, usually prompted a tendency to hold back until another pushed the conversation, but down under that shy countenance was something much deeper, a man of definite inner feelings and one who would respond in any emergency. The youngest among the keepers attached to the station, he was obviously an honest and straightforward individual.

We got to talking about the foghorns and he informed me that in many storms, rocks and seaweed torn loose by the rampaging seas had clogged the trumpet openings so that no sound was emitted. The task of clearing the trumpets was a dangerous occupation and sometimes, due to breaching seas, it would be days before anyone could climb up to dig the debris from the openings.

Continuing my foggy tour, I wandered down to the derrick house and found George there greasing and oiling the machinery. The derrick mast and boom showed the effects of hard usage and abuse by the weather. Many of the metal fittings were red with rust, including the iron wheel that swung from the boom. The winch and hoist were similar to what one might find on the deck of an old cargo ship.

George informed me that the boom had been carried away several times in storms and had to be replaced, necessitating the rigging of a breeches buoy as a temporary means of transporting personnel and supplies on and off the rock. George was the oldest member of our crew, both in years and from the standpoint of service. He was a rugged individual and not too well educated. Everything he had learned had come from hard experience, and I had the feeling he might have had a rather unhappy home life as a child. He seemed to regret the fact that his education had been neglected, and even though he was the potentate of the rock, I reasoned that his wife was probably the ruler in their household.

More than the others, George looked upon me as a necessary evil, a lame-duck addition for spelling off the others only. He was rather reluctant to explain the derrick's operation and always made a special point of keeping me away from that duty. He reasoned that only the more skilled were capable of operating the levers. After my initial dunking I was content to leave things just that way so as not to be accused of forcing "water baptism" on another.

Despite George's seeming dislike for me, I couldn't help respecting him for his abilities. Crude as they were, he got the job done and evidently his superiors were not concerned about his butchering of the king's English in his reports and in correspondence with the district headquarters.

George griped constantly about the lack of attention given to the rock. And rightfully so, for virtually all the equipment in the place was ancient compared to shoreside lighthouses. The Coast Guard considered it the most costly station in the district to maintain, repairs coming only after storm damage impeded the operation of the station.

Still, as George informed me, Tillamook Light was the only local navigation aid not extinguished or greatly reduced in intensity during the early years of the war when it was feared the Japanese would invade. In fact, the Nipponese submarine that shelled Fort Stevens, in 1942, was undoubtedly guided by its light. It was the first shelling of mainland U.S. Territory by a foreign power since the Revolution. Fortunately there were no casualties.

I asked why Tillamook kept shining its light.

"Better of two evils," said George. "Better risk a shellin' than have a ship smash the rock." I couldn't help agreeing, for any vessel striking Tillamook Rock would undoubtedly have been totaled and her entire crew wiped out.

The day was full of surprises. Later that afternoon when the fog had subsided somewhat, I was at the west or bitter end of the rock, the place where savage seas often tore off fragments of basalt and drove them into the structure. Climbing outside the railing but hanging tightly with one hand, I looked down the perpendicular wall some 90 feet, and there to my surprise was a huge whale, the like of which I had never before seen. He was evidently rubbing the barnacles from his broad back and side, lying virtually immobile about two feet under the surface. The seas had subsided, calmed by the stillness of the foggy atmosphere.

As I was yet to learn, it wasn't uncommon for whales and sharks to visit the base of the rock, under proper conditions, for a turn at rubbing off irritating crustaceans.

In my excitement I told the others of my discovery, but they showed little enthusiasm for something so common to them. So I decided to get a little action out of the critter. Finding a large 50-pound hunk of rock a previous storm had torn loose, I crept back over the railing to the target site. The ocean was pearl-gray except directly below me where it had taken on an iridescent hue, the brine clear as crystal glass.

Zeroing in, I braced myself, one leg hanging behind the railing so as not to join the company of the whale. Down plummeted the missile, gathering speed as it went. I had only meant to scare the mammoth mammal, but the bomb split the water and struck it on the back of the head—a direct hit. With the suddenness of a lightning flash, a massive forked-tail became airborne. Like a great juggernaut, thrashing, writhing, the leviathan broke the surface and charged the basaltic mass, ramming its snout with a sickening thud. I thought the entire rock would be decapitated, when suddenly the whale disappeared into the depths. The ocean was a foamy mass, punctured by whirlpools and masses of effervescent bubbles.

When the monster surfaced a second time, the jaw was wide open. Giant fountains of water erupted from its blowhole as the barnacle-covered back arched above the boiling maelstrom. As if searching out its foe, the whale's desperate antics continued for nearly fifteen minutes. I could only imagine the fury and anger of that swimming tornado. Glad to be well out of its range and preferring not to be a second Jonah, I watched with amazement. Never relaxing, the mammal propelled itself at furious speeds. Each time the frenzied battering ram passed below me, its proportions seemed to increase in size.

Though this was one of the most exciting moments of my life, I had nobody with whom to share it. The whale, exhausted but still furious, finally gave up and vanished into the deep, probably never again to return to that most inhospitable of all ocean bastions.

My experience prompted my interest in finding out more about such huge creatures. I learned that my victim was one of the great California Grays that make their trek from the Bering Sea to Mexico's west coast annually, the longest migration of any species of whale—an eight-months' round trip, some 7,000 to 11,000 miles. Among these nomads of the sea are a few stragglers, which for reasons unknown, fail to make the entire migration, remaining instead off the Oregon coast. Grays are generally between 45 and 50 feet in length and more than a ton per foot. Barnacles and skin pigments give these baleen whales a mottled hue. It is claimed they need little rest or food on their long migrations. In the months to follow I was to see a great number of leviathans basking about off the rock on their unusual travels, comparable to the salmon that roam the Pacific on a three-year cycle and then return to the place of their birth to spawn.

That night at dinner I mentioned my experience once again but it seemed to fall on deaf ears, drowned out by agitation over the foghorn. The option of when to turn the signal off or on rested with the keeper on duty. But as I was soon to find out, in isolated lighthouses the argument over the foghorn caused more heated discussions and even outright fights than did anything else. Nobody liked to listen to that mournful call anymore than necessary and it was obvious that those long, protracted periods of foghorn blasting were nerve-racking.

In the station I found file copies of letters sent to the authorities by former keepers asking for transfer to another lighthouse. Complaints for the most part involved maintenance of the fog-signal equipment and its operation. Most of the early lighthouse keepers chose their occupation knowing full well they would be removed from the mainstream and given to separation. Many faced their abstract life well but there existed many differences between the parties involved, some of which ended in dramatic climax and others in bitter stalemate. Case in point: A letter of complaint written December 19, 1906:

Commander
Inspector 13th L.H. District
Portland, Oregon

Sir:

You will please transfer me to some other station or relieve me from any further duty on Tillamook Rock Light Station. The first assistant Keeper Mr. Dalgren and I are constantly quarreling over the work and hours of work and conditions in general.

The boilers (for the foghorn, steam operated) have not been cleaned for a long time and are now in very filthy condition. Mr. Dalgren allows that this station is accorded certain privileges on account of water not granted other stations, and for that reason the boilers are not given the same consideration here as elsewhere. However, there is now and has been for some time an abundant supply of water, consequently there is no reasonable excuse why the boilers should not be cleaned.

The water columns and gauge cocks are troublesome on account of foreign matter, which is itself evidence that boilers should have received attention.

It is customary to wait till the atmosphere has become thick or foggy before lighting fires under boilers, and then rush things. It usually takes about 90 minutes to generate steam at 70 pounds pressure per square inch.

Mr. Dalgren insists it is none of my business how things are managed. However, as I have some experience in the case and management of steam boilers, I refuse to be party to any such practice. It is absolutely impossible that Mr. Dalgren and I agree under such conditions.

Very Respectfully
Michael Bergen, Fourth Assistant Keeper

Under the old U.S. Lighthouse Service, the principal or head keeper had somewhat the same authority as a shipmaster, all personnel being under Civil Service. When the keeper-in-charge was absent, the First Assistant took over the helm, as was the case here with Dalgren.

Bergen's letter went unanswered for many weeks, but when the answer did come, it was not addressed to Bergen but to the station's chief keeper, William T. Langlois, and was signed by P.J. Werlich, Commander USN, Lighthouse Inspector. It advised that the complaining fourth assistant should acquaint himself with the "rules and regulations governing the Light-House Establishment on file at the station," and "henceforth send his letter through the keeper-in-charge," in this case, Mr. Langlois.

Contentions between the two assistant keepers continued to fester, finally reaching the boiling point. They challenged each other to a gun duel. After writing a second, and this time, frantic letter through the chief keeper, Bergen was finally granted his transfer. It came just in time, for it was certain that blood would have been spilled. Fortunately the Tillamook Rock version of the "quick draw" never came off.

I was learning fast the meaning of the old proverb, "familiarity breeds contempt," and the fact that individuals who were slow to anger, resourceful and quiet made by far the best lighthouse keepers in isolated places. The personnel problems were considerable at Tillamook through the years. Sometimes differences ended in fisticuffs. In August, 1929, a letter from the Superintendent of Lighthouses, Portland, Oregon, was received by the principal keeper at Tillamook. It read:

> On the monthly report of your station for the month of January, 1929, there is a notation relative to differences between two keepers at your station. No reference is made to the parties concerned. It is requested that you advise the names of the individuals together with the circumstances connected with the differences for the records of this office and to prevent any reflection on keepers at the station not concerned in the difficulty.

The request was immediately answered by the station's first assistant, Teofil Milkowski, one of the individuals involved in the fracas:

Dear Sir:

The head keeper was absent and me being the first assistant I tried to do my part. Now the trouble was between me and Mr. Ben W. Franklin.

Now this is what it was about. He had runned the engine for at least a half an hour and no sound of blast was heard so I wanted to know the reason for that and why the chart didn't show that it was blowed down, as he was on watch at the time. And when I took the chart to him he got mad and began to call me all kinds of bad names. Now this is what I asked of him. Now you fellows are both here why don't this chart show that it was blowed down here. Mr. Wheeler and Mr. Franklin were both there so I didn't want trouble. I started out of the kitchen and Mr. Franklin struck me from the back on my ear and I turned around and he grabbed me so we went at it and I gave him plenty.

Six months later, after a continuous lack of communication (the silent treatment) between the keepers, Franklin was transferred to another station.

A former lighthouse superintendent, some years ago, revealed the results of a miserable misunderstanding between the keepers of Alaska's isolated Cape Hinchinbrook Lighthouse. On making his annual visit he found the three attendants totally at odds with one another. It all began when one desired his potatoes fried and the other mashed. In an endeavor to settle the dispute, the third party, the head keeper, almost got a truce in the culinary dispute when another fracas over a missing ring erupted. Again the head keeper intervened but this time he went too far and also got involved. The final result was three estranged keepers totally isolated from the rest of the world, refusing to communicate, not even imparting a single word for six long months, each standing his watch and cooking his own meals in complete solitude. Such incidents caused some keepers to lose their sanity.

The age-old saying for the lighthouse attendant in isolated stations was, "Never let your mind wander beyond the line of duty."

# CHAPTER 4

# THE HISTORIC PAST

In an isolated lighthouse the rapid pace of life on the mainland is virtually forgotten. In place of jangled nerves and ulcers, the principal ailment is melancholy.

One night, after putting a jewel-like glow on the light lens at the expense of five rags and two tired arms, I wandered up the narrow staircase to the attic library to browse through the ancient collection of literature. The sagging shelves labored with books and periodicals from bygone years. Apparently none of the collection had been discarded since the incarceration of the first lighthouse keeper. Every subject imaginable was contained in dust-covered volumes donated down through the years by sympathetic seashore humanitarians.

One glance at the vast collection told me the lighthouse did not belong to the Book-of-the-Month Club, and that funds for magazine subscriptions had terminated with the era of the Model T Ford. The musty room had a definite air of quaintness, both to sight and nostril, and if one did not mind an inch of dust or a network of cobwebs scattered sparingly about, it had a bit of the romantic atmosphere as well. Those books had been read and re-read by keepers long since gone to their deserved rest. Before the inception of telephone and radio, the volumes had probably been worth their weight in gold. I was almost afraid to disturb them. Each time I touched one, a cloud of dust erupted as though a curse had been placed upon it.

In one corner of the room was a neat stack of old lighthouse records and logbooks, many of which were preserved from pre-century years. As I examined the contents of their moldy pages, I soon became absorbed and found myself reading far into the night. Those early excerpts told of the staggering toll of shipwreck on and around the mouth of the Columbia River, a primary factor in the decision to construct the lighthouse. In early years that disreputable river-bar approach had been the bane of mariners.

Youthful Uncle Sam must have had a touch of Scotch ancestry in those days (back in 1878) because he decided that $50,000 should be ample for the erection of a light south of the Columbia River entrance. The Solons were of course unfamiliar with the peculiarities of the Oregon coast. Originally it was decided to place the lighthouse on the shore, atop Tillamook Head, but the cost of building and maintaining a switch-back road to its 1000-foot summit, and the persistent fog and low-hanging clouds at that level, made the plan prohibitive.

Then along came Major G.I. Gillespie, of the Army Corps of Engineers. His opinion was that the lighthouse should be built at sea, and his suggestion was Tillamook Rock. This met with immediate opposition, for hitherto the crag had been unconquered by human resourcefulness and daring, and was considered unconquerable. Meanwhile, the loss of property and lives continued to increase along the coast on either side of the Columbia River entrance.

Public demand left the Lighthouse Board no alternative but to proceed with their plans. With the preliminaries completed, H.S. Wheeler, district superintendent of lighthouse construction, took over the reins. He had a long title for the short years one usually spent in such a rugged occupation, for he, like the others in his profession, was a versatile and courageous individual. It was his assignment to gain a foothold on Tillamook Rock, reputedly never before approached by man. Even the coastal Indians had kept their distance from the crag, believing it to be cursed by their gods. Wheeler was ready to tackle the job on receiving notice from the U.S. Lighthouse Board that it had officially sanctioned construction of a light station atop Tillamook Rock. All other probable sites had been ruled out.

Meantime, preparations were underway at Astoria to facilitate pending construction work. When June of 1879 rolled around, the weather changed its personality, and the engineers were encouraged by the first promising prospect of landing on the rock. Wheeler was taken to the site by the U.S. Revenue Cutter *Thomas Corwin*, and put over the side in a boat a safe distance from the rock. As he came abreast of the massive monolith, he ruled out any chance of landing. Though the ocean was moderate, the breakers pounded against the bastion unmercifully, and whirlpools and eddies swept about the area. All Wheeler could do was reconnoiter.

A week later he was commissioned to stand watch near Astoria and report the first favorable break in the weather, so that another attempt could be made. Furthermore, he was instructed not to return to his headquarters until his mission had been accomplished. After a long and weary vigil, day and night, the indomitable engineer finally greeted a dawn many weeks later that gave promise of a rare, windless day, clearing atmosphere, and unusually calm seas. With a selected boat crew he shoved off, but once near Tillamook it was the same old story—a running swell, and curling, twisting breakers sending icy fingers up the sides of the black rock. But Wheeler would be balked no longer.

At great risk the boat was brought up along the eastern exposure, the only side that did not have perpendicular walls, and two sailors were ordered to get up on it in the best fashion they could. Time after time, the poised men would crouch, ready to spring, but it was a case of intricate timing as the boat would rear up on a 10-foot swell and then drop like a 1000-pound anchor. They were gradually being subdued by fear until Wheeler demanded that they jump. Leaping with every ounce of spring in their bodies, they landed safely, and in all probability were the first persons to do so. The next problem was to land the engineer's survey instruments, but as if incensed by this partial success, the seas grew in intensity and the boat had to stand off the rock to keep from being dashed to pieces. Fearing that they would be stranded, the men on the rock, paralyzed with fright, hurled themselves back into the frenzied waters and were pulled to safety by their lifelines.

Wheeler was bitterly disappointed. Realizing the inevitable risk in the undertaking, he himself determined to land alone. Thus, four days later, he put out again in a surfboat with a handful of men pulling the oars. The same method—that of bringing the boat in on the crest of a swell and then jumping to the rock—was chosen by the engineer. Crouching in the bow, he waited his opportunity. Up, up, up, the boat climbed and just as it reached its apex, Wheeler sprang and clawed his way on the slippery base of the rock. Then by means of lines, he attempted to get his survey instruments ashore, but each attempt was thwarted.

With the seas picking up, he waved the boat off and set about with his hand tape, running it from point to point over the sharp layers of precipitous basalt. Jotting down hurried notes without time for concentrated analysis, he finished the job and hailed the boat. After several anxious moments he leaped from his slippery perch directly into the confines of the craft, and though he was badly bruised, his mission was accomplished after six months of waiting. His feat, unofficially speaking, enlarged the explored land of the United States by perhaps half an acre, including kelp, barnacles, and seagrass.

Wheeler's report was considered, and the character of the lighthouse and apparatus decided upon by the Lighthouse Board. His survey further revealed that the only solution for chiseling a lighthouse foundation was to blast several feet of hard substance from the overhanging crest, which at that time was between 115 and 120 feet above normal water and had the shape of a clenched fist. This, of course, was a hard pill for the Lighthouse Board to swallow, since the amount allotted for the station already appeared like a child's allowance.

While government authorities wallowed under the usual amount of red tape, John R. Trewaves, master mason with years of experience erecting lighthouses off the walls of England, was summoned to make a construction survey. In all of the United Kingdom he had never approached such a spot as Tillamook

Left: North Head Lighthouse, near the north entrance of the Columbia River, has been sending its beams seaward since 1898. (E.A. Delanty photo) Right: The initial lighthouse in the Pacific Northwest was rugged Cape Disappointment, erected in 1856.

Even before the building of Tillamook Rock Lighthouse, a vintage navigation aid was provided at the south entrance of the Columbia River. The Point Adams Lighthouse was erected in 1875 and operated until 1899. The extension of the south jetty diminished its effectiveness, and in 1912 the government ordered it burned to the ground.

The first Columbia River Lightship was the *No. 50*, seen here as it was hauled across the spit toward Bakers Bay after being driven ashore in an 1899 gale. (U.S. Coast Guard photo)

Another of the lightships that did duty off the entrance to the Columbia River was the *No. 93*, seen here at the Coast Guard repair base.

Rock. Destiny willed that he would never build another lighthouse, for he was drowned on September 18, 1879, while trying to run the gauntlet. His desperate effort to gain a foothold on the rock resulted in a bleeding corpse, which was sucked into the depths and never returned.

Fear of a similar fate grew in the hearts of the others and when the news of Trewaves's death reached the mainland, it riled the public to such a pitch that they frantically urged abandonment of the project. Lighthouse authorities, however, pressed the enterprise with unabated vigor before public opinion should sway the minds of would-be laborers being sought for the construction work.

Charles A. Ballantyne, a robust, intelligent builder with leadership talent, was chosen to succeed John Trewaves, in the role of superintendent of construction for the lighthouse. He was aware of the mammoth task confronting him, but tackled it with fervor on the promise of a handsome bonus. The first obstacle to hurdle was lining up eight skilled quarrymen who would not be taken in by caustic town gossip concerning the undertaking. Little did he realize the power of adverse comment until he attempted to recruit prospects from local ranks. Negative answers rang in his ears, and he was forced to fan out over the countryside to round up his crew. When his recruiting was completed, he had orders to proceed to Astoria with his party, where they would be transported directly to the rock, along with provisions and supplies. Unfortunately, there was a proverbial fly in the ointment when Ballantyne and his men reached the river port in the fall of 1879.

The seasonal gales had commenced early, rendering approach to the rock impossible, and there was no alternative but to house his party until favorable conditions existed. The construction engineer had no way of knowing whether it would be a matter of days or months; meantime, his brain was taxed as to how the quarrymen could be spared the talk of the town. Once turned loose, they would head for the saloons to get acquainted, and what they listened to would turn them against work on the rock. So Ballantyne corralled his charges on the outskirts of town and hurried here and there making arrangements for putting them up at a vacated lightkeeper's dwelling at Cape Disappointment (across the river and high atop an ocean cape). They would be away from all but a few government employees who would be instructed to play up the merits of the pending project.

As it turned out, the unsuspecting quarrymen were gullible; and away from pernicious influences, their stock in the enterprise rose considerably. But time was of the essence, and when the days began to drag into weeks, they became restless, bored and argumentative, trying to figure out the reason for the protracted delay. Twenty-six days passed before the revenue cutter finally anchored off the inside of the cape and took aboard Ballantyne and his party for transit out to the rock.

The ship was moored to a previously planted buoy and a boat was put over the side for a spine-tingling landing effort. When the quarrymen took but one look at the rock, its fearsome character caused lumps in their throats, for the breakers were rushing up its ragged walls, whipping spray in every direction and causing massive whirlpools at their offset. It was then that each wished he had pursued such a trade as a shoe salesman or a farmer. The sides of the protuberance dropped plumb into the sea, the lead giving readings from 96 to 250 feet, and at a glance they saw that the rock was split in two by a narrow fissure where the seas drove in like express trains, exploding with ear-shattering roars, and shooting skyward in great geysers.

Despite ceaseless attempts to land the men, over a period of six hours, only four managed to gain the rock and they only after the boat sprang a leak and smashed its gunwales. Then by means of block, tackle and lines, the little band managed with great difficulty to haul up hammers, drills, iron ringbolts, a small stove and an abundance of canvas, the mere necessities for survival and protection from the pounding seas. Some provisions were floated in by casks and hauled up on the lower climbs, but long before dusk, in the face of rising seas, the surfboat was compelled to retreat to the cutter.

The conquering party set to work building their shelter, yet it was five more days before the seas moderated and the remaining four members could be landed after a seven-hour wait in an open boat. With the newcomers came barrels of blasting powder and other essentials.

Less than three days after the second landing, the inhabitants were visited by a gale which scattered its wet fury across the rock, drenching everything and everyone, from above and below. The shocks of the titanic waves, packing the punch of a dynamo, covered the rock like a blanket over a bed. The men were terrified but soon became inured to their fate, for it was but a preliminary of things to come. The blasting powder was wet, the food soaked, and an abundance of salty brine had mixed with the fresh water supply. What was worse, all the sleeping blankets were wet clear through.

The difficulty of landing supplies had already been evidenced on previous occasions and it became obvious that other methods would have to be employed, else future shipments be lost in transit, causing work delays and hunger for the intrepid ones. To alleviate this danger, an ingenious plan was adopted at Tillamook Rock. It involved the anchoring of a large ship at a point just far enough from the rock to keep it out of the dangerous waters; then rigging up a heavy rope between the mast of the ship and the top of the rock, drawing it taut, and devising a traveler to run across its extent. In theory and practice it had been proven, so the task of making a 4½-inch hawser secure between the two given points was undertaken. When the quarrymen retrieved their end of the rope, it was anchored firmly and constituted the track. To this main line, was rigged a single block in such a way that it could move freely along the line, coupled with a heavy hook on which weights could be slung. At rock and ship, additional blocks and tackle were rigged, and passing through these blocks a line was made fast to the hook on the traveling block, allowing the traveler to be pulled freely in either direction. To this line was attached a breeches buoy to convey the workmen.

Though the ride above the sea was usually a rough one, full of thrills, suspense and submersions, all agreed that it was far superior to attempting a landing by boat. Principal drawback was that the vessel responded to the pulsating waves, alternately

drawing the cable taut and again allowing it to sag, so that the
man in transit would be dragged hundreds of feet through the
freezing water to spring back into the air and vibrate at a high
altitude like a yoyo on a string. But the rugged individuals didn't
grumble too much about their unceremonious immersions, especially if they were coming off the rock. When going the other
way, they cursed violently, for the little cook stove was the only
supply of warmth.

Landings were frequently the basis of wagers as to how many
times those in transit would be immersed. Despite such a hazardous operation, many laughs were forthcoming. One case stood
out among the others, that of a beefy 300-pound laborer named
Gruber. He was just too fat to get into the breeches buoy, and
regardless of three men grunting and groaning in an effort to
squeeze him in, it was as useless as trying to put a marble through
the eye of a needle. To all parties concerned it appeared as if
Ballantyne would have to send his new recruit back home.

But the engineer did not give up so easily, for laborers were
next to impossible to obtain. He signaled the master of the steamer to lash Gruber on top of the breeches buoy so that they could
drag him up to the rock, if need be. At such a suggestion the cor-
pulent individual became tremulous. He wasn't going to be
trussed up on a frail conveyance to be dragged through the sea, or
snapped up in the air, with a chance of the thing breaking under
his bulk, not him, not Gruber. He didn't relish being handled like
a cord of wood when even the supplies were landed in casks to
keep them dry. Against such protestations nothing remained but
to take the reluctant hand back to Astoria where the Lighthouse
Service could fit him with two giant-sized life preservers which,
sewed together, made a perfect fit about his waist. Next, the
breeches buoy was altered and the fat man was returned to the
site on the revenue cutter. So long had Gruber dwelled on the
possible perils of landing that he now refused to get into the
breeches buoy. Ballantyne was beside himself, and to assure the
raw hand that it was as simple as falling off a log, he had the
traveler brought to the rock, where Ballantyne himself jumped
into the buoy and moved across the abyss to show his recruit the

safety of the method. But Ballantyne's plan backfired; the cable was slack and the ship rolled heavily, dragging him through the water most of the way, and sometimes several feet under.

The fat boy would have none of it and demanded to be taken back to Astoria at once. The construction boss shed his rough exterior and turned to diplomacy and persuasion, but it got him nowhere. Then he stormed and raged, all to no avail, until in desperation he suggested the use of a bo's'n's chair, which would allow the big man more freedom in transit. After the chair was rigged up to the specifications of the hesitant individual, he agreed to try it. Trepidation again plagued him, but once they got him to sit down in the chair bundled in his life jackets, they cast him loose against his protests. To Gruber's surprise and everyone else's too, he was the first man to land on the rock without so much as wetting the soles of his shoes.

Next came the task of getting the segments of the derrick to the rock—a long, tedious undertaking which demanded human brawn and mental strain. A maze of ropes, hawsers, cables, blocks and tackle was used, and success was achieved. The derrick was ultimately equipped with a long boom that could drop a cable down to the deck of the steamer, making unnecessary a transit by block and tackle over the treacherous waters.

Ballantyne and his doughty band faced another obstacle in the warring sea lions, which for decades had been in command of the lower confines of the rock. They scaled its weathered east side in large numbers, some of them managing to gain the summit. Never had their haunts been disturbed until man came with his tools and blasting powder to cause loose rock to rain down on them, sometimes injuring their young. Occasionally the infuriated mammals would make attacks on their adversaries, but the construction gang controlled the upper climbs so the sea lions were ultimately forced to retreat. They deserted the islet in one great body to take up lodging on another isolated bastion farther down the coast.

Tillamook Rock, which had withstood the pounding of the Pacific for a million years, was soon subject to a new kind of destructive agent administered by the hands of man—blasting powder. With the tremendous overhanging western slope, the job facing the construction crew was leveling a foundation area by dropping the summit of the rock from 120 to 91 feet. The rock here was scarred and distorted in weird formations from the scouring action of the waves which had eroded the outer portions, leaving the hard substance in the form of sharp ridges and knife-like crevices. The outer sections of the rock formed the danger areas, for with the slightest jar, landslides would begin. On the other hand, the tough, inner basalt was hard and excellent for a lighthouse foundation. To guard against damaging landslides and so as not to dislodge the solidarity of the heart of the rock, the most powerful blasts moved no more than 130 cubic yards at one time. Even with the slow operations, every muffled explosion was flirtation with death, for sometimes the outer crust converged on the men like broken ice in a spring thaw.

Other problems also delayed the drilling and blasting, namely the elements of weather—rain, fog, and wind. Nevertheless, Tillamook Rock became a minor smoking volcano. Often, blasting powder became wet and charges failed to go off. Again, drilling-holes would be filled with sea water. The men hovered around the crest of the rock with no level place to stand on when hiding from the blasts. To make possible such a spine-tingling performance, huge iron ring-bolts were driven into the walls of the rock for handholds and footholds. For drilling holes, a foot rope was run between two of the ring-bolts, and a crude staging placed on which to work. Many of the stagings were more than a hundred feet above the ocean, and the men were compelled to swing crazily in heavy winds, constantly soaked by spray—one hand for the government, the other for themselves.

When the day's task of blasting and drilling was over, there was no warm barracks to go to, only a crude canvas shelter in the form of an A-frame tent, cramped and uncomfortable. Of these quarters Ballantyne's journal stated:

> It was rather disagreeable in our tent, it being six by sixteen feet with a horizontal ridge pole about four feet six inches from the ground. The tent, which is our only shelter,

holds the ten of us. We always do our cooking on the lee side and shift with the wind direction.

The construction boss was lenient in his analysis of the conditions, for he did not mention the fact that the tenants were forced to crawl instead of walk, and had to eat and cook in those miserable quarters which hung on the side of the rock like a seashell. Winds lashed the tent, causing the canvas to flap wildly, and spray frequently swept over it, drenching the inside and often threatening to carry the entire shelter into the ocean. Sometimes the cookstove was filled with salt water and the supplies soaked through.

Ballantyne was not only superintendent of the work but was also house mother to the little army of die-hards. He was always ready for any contingency that arose. Arguments, hatreds, homesickness, loneliness, privation—each in turn was suffered by his men, but he administered to their needs like one possessed of superhuman endurance.

As fall turned into winter, supply ships could no longer come near the rock. The last vessel to land materials slipped her anchor and made a run to safety in the face of rising seas. With winter came the end of the old year and the beginning of the new. One went out like a tiger, the other roared in like a lion. With each hour the ominous clouds took on a more sinister appearance. Rain pelted down and blasts howled in from the southwest.

For six days the wind blew until it reached hurricane proportions. Until then the men had worked, drenched to the skin, barely able to keep their feet against the force of the wind. Finally, Ballantyne one day gave the command to cease work, for fear his crew would be swept to violent death. More ring-bolts were embedded in the rock and everything lashed down securely, including the wooden shack which had been built for housing. The men worked with a will, for the entire Oregon coast as far as the eye could reach was a seething disturbance of white, yeasty foam, tormented by the savage winds—and Tillamook Rock appeared to be the vortex and the primary target of the storm's fury.

With night coming on, the quarrymen took to their shelter, cold, wet, and miserable. Already the salt water was flowing under the door and leaking through the roof. The sea's roar was so deafening that shouting proved the only means of communication. Fear gripped the hearts of the men. By the light of the storm lamp, their moving lips suggested silent prayers. Even their leader had to suppress his anxieties over a situation that appeared hopeless. Nevertheless, he insisted that those in his charge remain in their bunks and attempt to get a little rest. But the rock trembled under each watery onslaught, and sleep was almost impossible; fear made it even more so.

At two in the morning there came a thunderous crash, louder than all the others. The men sat erect in their bunks, petrified, as if waiting momentarily to be carried into the depths. Ballantyne warned against any of them stepping foot from the dwelling to investigate, for danger lurked at every crevice on the old rock. But the suspense was more than they could endure; finally the foreman grabbed the storm lantern and went outside. Before he stepped a foot from the door, the breaching seas hurled him back and the wind lashed him against the shack. But not to be denied, he waited for two hours, then crawled up the rotten crust of the rock.

Gone for only two minutes, he staggered back bruised and exhausted to announce that everything was blacker than the ace of spades, and that he could see nothing. So all hands remained helpless in their bunks as the seas tore off large pieces of rock and dropped them on the shelter roof. The fragments increased with each breaker, and finally began to open large holes through which sea water poured at will. The canvas of the original shelter was ordered out and lashed across the roof to hold the Pacific out of the barracks. When at long last, dawn broke, all eyes focused on the reason for the terrible crash. The seas had descended on the storehouse, lifted it from its fittings and carried it into the sea, along with building materials and the fresh-water tank. Only one scant pile of goods had miraculously escaped the icy fangs of the breakers.

The gale continued although the seas abated somewhat. To keep his men from going mad, Ballantyne forced them to work a few hours each day in spite of scant food rations. Not until January 18 was the revenue steamer able to fight her way to the lee of the rock to learn the fate of the isolated souls. A surfboat with volunteers was put over the side and brought in daringly near the rock to learn that all the storm victims were still alive, but subsisting on rations of hardtack, coffee and bacon. A promise was made that the steamer would send provisions as soon as possible.

After one hundred more terrifying hours, the hurricane showed further signs of breaking; then, like groundhogs, the men came out to search for morsels of food and to rig up patches of canvas in an effort to catch rainwater. The best the relief ship could do was to gain a position a half mile from the disaster scene. The gaunt band of lighthouse builders peered over the storm-tossed waters as if they were seeing a mirage, and it might just as well have been, for they could do nothing but continue their tormenting wait.

The master of the steamer was helpless, for he well knew a landing in such a sea was a virtual impossibility. Putting a boat over the side had been short of suicide; so he concentrated his efforts on getting a line into the hands of the rock-bound clan. First he attempted to get a light rope to the rock, made fast to an empty cask, but before it drifted halfway it was smashed to pieces. Not easily defeated, the captain and his crew then devised a plan whereby a box kite made from a bed sheet and two barrel staves could be sent skyward with the wind. From the ship's crow's nest this unorthodox invention was soon soaring toward the rock. To the onlookers it must have appeared like a Rube Goldberg gadget, but it proved the plain and simple answer, paying out a light line that reached the eager hands of the desperate victims. This enabled them to haul in a heavier line which was made fast between the steamer's foremast and the rock, allowing supplies and dry clothing to bridge the watery gap. Later the lighthouse tender arrived and managed to get additional supplies landed.

Meanwhile, efforts were being pressed to enlist more men to aid in the construction of the lighthouse, but adverse propaganda had rendered the effort well-nigh hopeless. But more hands were urgently needed to rectify the situation, and rumor persisted that crimps were engaged who specialized in the illicit art of shanghaiing. Such heinous individuals had a notorious reputation around the saloons and flophouses, from Astoria to Portland, for having filled the empty berths of many windjammers. Word that they were on the prowl leaked out and the local dives suddenly showed a decline in business. Pickings proved slim and in desperation the crimps slipped across the Columbia to prey on unsuspecting individuals in riverbank villages. Several days later, so it was said, a small sling load of unwilling victims shook off their stupors atop the rock and wondered if they had died and gone to hell.

With more hands, fresh provisions, and improved shelter, plus a few days of mild weather, the project showed its first real progress.

Preparations were made to better handle heavy building materials. Experiences with the former landing gear had at times proved disastrous and the experts of the local Lighthouse Service were summoned together to solve the problem. The result was a steam-operated derrick and hoist with an exceptionally long boom, designed to stretch out over the water like the neck of a giraffe, with the lifting power of a team of elephants. First experiments with the boom under a heavy burden almost caused its dislodgement, but by deeply embedding anchorages of supporting stiff legs, that obstacle was overcome. Further kid-glove treatment prompted the innovation to exceed all expectations and hastened the laying of the lighthouse cornerstone by several weeks. Not only were the derrick and boom used for heavy-lift materials, they soon became the mode for all transfer of personnel and supplies as well. . . .The cornerstone read:

TILLAMOOK ROCK LIGHT STATION
June 24, 1880

Early-day oil painting (1880) depicting Tillamook Rock being supplied by the revenue cutter *Corwin*. The painter took some liberties with the lighthouse but captured a mood.

This postal card illustrating the lighthouse around the turn of the century gives it a touch of the romantic.

And from that day hence, huge squares of granite rose block by block as the structure took shape. The utmost in construction skill was poured into the lighthouse along with such materials as iron, lumber, brick, concrete and plaster. The walls were as thick as those of the mightiest of fortresses. Even with milder weather the ocean often continued its vengeance and the men cursed the fate that had deposited them on the rock. But they pursued their task, encouraged by the protective walls that rose around them.

Summer faded into fall and the dwelling and tower progressed well. Then came winter again, and with it that regrettable night of January 3, 1881.

The usual dirty weather had closed about the rock, when suddenly the construction boss entered the dwelling, claiming to have sighted running lights below the walls of the crag. By the dim flicker from the stove the others stared at him, wondering if he was cracking under the strain. Nevertheless, they filed outside, climbed to the highest vantage point, and peered into the blackness. There was no mistaking that eerie glow of port and starboard lanterns against the livid tempest. As they listened to the intonations of the sea, there came above the roar a discordant command: "Hard Aport!" followed by the creaking and rattling of rigging and turning yardarms, suggesting that the command had been promptly heeded. That the ship, whatever her identity, was on the horns of a dilemma was a foregone conclusion. Accordingly, the construction crew was ordered to build the largest bonfire possible near the lighthouse foundation to warn the ship away from certain disaster.

The men sprang into action, kindled a fire and fed it with anything and everything that would burn, until it shot up pillars of orange flame. Lanterns were then placed about sparingly at other vantage points until at last the running lights of the ship disappeared in the murk. But whatever feeling of satisfaction that had come to the lighthouse crew that night faded the following morning when a woeful sight greeted their eyes. Jutting solemnly above the surface inshore was a mizzen topmast, the only vestige of a ship, a grim reminder of death. The little party on the rock faced the reality that their warning had been heeded, but perhaps unfamiliarity with the coast on the part of the ship's master, or an erratic compass needle, deflected by the proximity of land, had caused the square-rigger to pursue the wrong course and crash into the perpendicular walls of Tillamook Head.

Later it was learned that the wreck was the British bark *Lupatia*, inbound for the Columbia River from Japan. There was only one survivor, and he could neither talk nor write, for that survivor was a dog, a bedraggled Australian shepherd pup which limped along the beach whining from thirst and hunger. His ship-mates were either trapped in the confines of the sunken ship or lay lifeless among the boulders on the beach.

"God!" exclaimed the master-mason, "if only the light had been shining, those poor devils could have gained safe waters." He looked back at the unfinished lighthouse with a sense of dis-satisfaction. "Back to work, men!" he ordered.

Flying the British flag, the 1,300 ton *Lupatia*, at the time of the tragedy, was skippered by her first officer, B.H. Raven, who had taken command after his brother, Captain Irvine Raven, died at sea, nine days out of Antwerp. The skipper's wife was aboard but debarked when the vessel reached Japan.

Departing Hiogo (Japan) for the Columbia in ballast, the *Lupatia* was to have loaded wheat on the river. She had been part of the Columbia River grain fleet since 1878, and in every sense was a splendid commercial sailing vessel. Though her entire crew of 16 perished, most of the bodies were recovered (12 washing up on the beach), but the perilous area of the wreck made it difficult for the searching party to find a suitable burial ground. The bodies were dragged a mile or so and placed in a single plot with-out services, the tombstone being the remnants of the wreck, which was soon leveled by the pounding surf.

The frightened pup, the lone survivor, eyes swollen and shak-ing from the cold, found a sympathetic owner, a friend of the Ravens' at Astoria. The befriended pooch lived out its years, happy with its new master. The following lines are a memorial to the tragedy of the *Lupatia*:

### Ode to the Lupatia

Why did you fail, O ship of sail,
There mangled on the reef?
Why did you fain the bounding main—
For now you've come to grief.

No hope in sight all through the night,
The dismal, abysmal dark—
You missed the light, O what a sight,
You came far short of the mark.

In too far, short of the bar,
The human hand has failed,
Rudder bent, wheel is rent
To rock and sand you're nailed.

No route to ply, 'tis here you die,
Your coffin closed so tight—
No more to roam through ocean foam,
Your crew has lost the fight.

Why did you fail O ship of sail—
Your bones to bleach in brine,
No star-filled sky to steer you by,
No gravestone—no hope—no shrine.

A few of the construction workers who had refused to believe a ship was actually out in the storm, repined in the aftermath of the incident. One, learning of the death of the entire ship's company, was quoted as saying, "If we had only believed our ears. If we had just shouted, made some kind of loud noise! Exploded a stick or two of dynamite! We might have warned them off. It was tough looking at the remains of that ship day after day and realizing that we perhaps could have saved it. From that hour on, finishing the tower to get the light lit and the foghorn going was more than just a job."

The unfortunate tragedy throttled any elaborate lighthouse commissioning ceremonies. It did, however, tend to speed the moment when the first "wickie" (slang name for lighthouse keepers who trimmed the wicks) lit the lamp and placed the steam fog signal in operation.

On January 21, only three weeks after the shipwreck, the light was displayed for the first time, a primary seacoast light of the first order of the system of Fresnel. The long and difficult task, the danger, hardship and privation, were over at last. The lighthouse was completed after 575 working days and an expense of $123,493. The construction crew anxiously awaited their departure and willingly turned lock, stock and barrel over to the incoming keepers, led by principal keeper, Albert Roeder.

The newcomers were soon to experience the ugly nature of the rock, but they held stubbornly to their priority concern, to keep the gleaming, high-intensity beacon aglow and the big steam fog siren operative.

During a gale in January of 1883, fragments, torn loose from the rock by treacherous seas, knocked several large holes in the iron roof of the foghorn house. In December of 1886, a mass of concrete filling, weighing half a ton, was ripped loose by rampaging seas and thrown into the enclosure, causing serious damage 100 feet above the ocean. The original ventilators projecting through the roof were all damaged or flattened by watery battering rams. What remained had to be removed and the holes sealed over. An early marine railway for pulling surfboats up to the rock was totally eradicated by the stormy seas and never replaced.

In the severest storm of December, 1887, the keepers reported that seas continuously broke over the tower, 134 feet above the sea, smashing the lantern panes and flooding the interior rooms. December 9, 1894, saw great seas that breached the entire station, destroying thirteen lantern panes, chipping the lens, and tearing off weighty fragments of rock that punctured the roofs of the dwelling and foghorn house, pouring in gallons of salt water and quantities of debris. In the blow of 1897, the newly laid $6,000 telephone cable connecting the station with the shore, was cleanly severed.

The alarming cost of maintenance, repair and supply made the rock the most expensive item on the list of United States lighthouses. Around the seacoasts of the world it became known as the most treacherous of warning posts.

In October of 1912, the supply ship was unable to near the rock for more than seven weeks because of the persistent irascible seas. Here is an entry from the head keeper's log:

> I regret to state that on the evening of October 18, 1912, or on the morning of October 19th, we lost a portion of the west end of the rock, water and rocks coming over with so much noise we could not tell when, and did not know it had departed until the next morning when the sea went down, so we could go outside. At 12:35 a.m. on October 19th, the sea came up and broke one pane in the middle section of the lantern, which also put the light out and flooded the watch room, as well as the downstairs. To add to it all, the soot and ashes came out of the kitchen stove.
>
> At 12:50 a.m. we had the light burning again and a storm pane in for the rest of the night. The siren was running until the crash came, but making no regular blast on account of water filling the trumpet too fast. After getting the light burning we closed the fog signal down, as the wind hauled to westward and cleared the atmosphere somewhat. Shortly afterwards, when taking the siren out to clear it, I found it filled with rocks; therefore water could not get out 100 feet above the sea. I will also state that everyone under my charge worked hard and faithfully regardless of water and glass, everybody being drenched to the skin.

In 1913, another winter gale brought a shift in the wind with such suddenness that it caused an ugly cross-sea which sent waves barreling into the tower. So many rocks were hurled into the lighthouse that a gunboat firing a full broadside could not have done more damage. Panes of glass were shattered and prisms badly chipped. The onslaught lasted fifteen hours and the keepers actually believed that the lighthouse would be carried into the sea. The damage, all told, ran into thousands of dollars.

To this day, the continuity of destruction has never ceased, and never does a winter slip by without chalking up another scar on

About 1930, at low tide, just after supplies had been shipped to the rock. Note keepers on the landing platform.

One of the most familiar pictures of Tillamook Rock was among the files of the U.S. Lighthouse Service photos, and believed snapped in the 1920s. During the station's active service, only 226 persons signed the guest register. Two of the most unusual visitors were Wallace Hug and Jim O. Reed, who swam the perilous waters from Seaside to the rock in 1934.

Station railings, tanks and pipes were ripped out by huge flying fragments of rock at the height of the October 1934 storm.

Devastating seas pulled iron bolts—buried more than three feet in solid rock—from their anchorages, allowing the mast and boom to be swept from the rock.

its adversary. The rock is the loser and will be until the last chapter in its chronicle has been written.

A story of faithful duty gained the acclaim of the world in the North Pacific gale of October, 1934. Tremendous seas submerged the entire station during that blow, and fragments weighing more than a hundred pounds were thrown at phenomenal heights. Small fish and seaweed were deposited in the lantern room as the keepers tried desperately to erect storm shutters to hold back the sea. It was urgent that news of the damage reach headquarters immediately, since a temporary light, feeble in comparison and without flashing potential, would be confusing to tempest-driven ships. Then too, all of the landing gear, including the boom, had been carried into the sea, the station flooded, and heating pipes and vents broken.

The ingenuity of keeper Jenkins brought about a solution. With old spare parts lying around the lighthouse, he contrived a short-wave radio-sending apparatus. The mercy role fell to the lighthouse tenders *Rose* and *Manzanita*, which braved the Columbia bar and made their way to the rock against voluminous seas. They were compelled to wait several days before it was possible to land a repair crew and supplies. The heavy damage, amounting to more than $12,000, required months to complete and the two tenders made a series of voyages because of the prevailing sequence of adverse weather.

The entire account was published at length by the chief of the Lighthouse Service of Mexico, who translated and distributed copies to all lighthouse keepers in the Latin Americas, as an example of devotion and courage in keeping the light burning against overwhelming odds.

This is how the epic story of the October 21, 1934, storm unfolded: The Pacific was in one of its infuriated moods. Chief Keeper William Hill, who had put in a long tenure on the rock, had seldom ever faced such conditions. Pacific Northwest shores were being hammered with unprecedented fury, and totally exposed Tillamook Rock shouldered wind velocities up to 109 mph. Repeatedly submerged under avalanches of sea water, the lighthouse was receiving one of its most severe poundings, tons of

basalt being sheered off the west end of the rock while huge geysers erupted in the fissure at the southwest corner. Boulders and
debris broken from the mass were thrown clear up to the lantern,
134 feet above mean water, some weighing more than 60 pounds
crashing through the glass panes onto the lantern room floor.
Twelve panels were knocked out and the lens prisms shattered in
a million pieces. The keepers worked up to their waists in salt-
water as the seas pummelled the tower, sending torrents of water
down the circular staircase to flood the inside of the lighthouse.

The light was knocked out. An emergency standby lamp had to
be installed and protective panels inserted to help hold out the
sea water.

The courage of the keepers under extreme duress was outstand-
ing. Nobody slept; it was work 24 hours around the clock, and
worse yet, the station's only contact with the shore, the cable, had
been severed. No way could the keepers tell the world of their
problem. The telephone was dead.

To the rescue came the genius of Assistant Keeper Jenkins. An
experienced radio ham, he began working with bits and pieces of
the useless telephone, along with other items found in the fog
signal room. Putting his know-how to work, many hours later he
came up with a working short-wave set that could both send and
receive. As the storm raged on, a new radio station was born behind the massive stone walls of the lighthouse.

Next, Jenkins frantically spun the wave lengths, hoping to
establish contact with some dedicated ham. His efforts were
eventually rewarded. Paydirt was struck with an amateur in
Portland whose call letters were W7WR. After some hurried conversation, Jenkins and Hill asked the receiver to contact the
Portland depot of the Lighthouse Service, requesting assistance as
soon as possible because the station was a shambles.

The message was immediately relayed, which put the wheels in
action at lighthouse depots in both Portland and Astoria. Supplies
and equipment were hastily loaded aboard the faithful old lighthouse tender *Manzanita*, while at the same time lighthouse
authorities kept in constant touch with the U.S. Weather Bureau.
It was now October 26, five days since the giant seas had knocked

out the light at Tillamook. High winds and gargantuan seas still plagued the North Pacific. The forecaster predicted a slight lull but warned it would be followed by another solid front and that Tillamook Rock was again directly in its path. Despite the ominous report, there was no hesitation on the part of the *Manzanita* crew. E. C. Merrill, district lighthouse superintendent, and the light tender's first officer, Claude Asquith, would together land on the rock and make an on-the-spot inspection. Asquith was acting skipper of the *Manzanita*, while Captain Modeer was on leave.

Battling against terrific odds, the *Manzanita* crossed the Columbia bar almost standing on end in the mammoth swells. But this tried and tested vessel, which had challenged all the reefs and obstructions on the West Coast, rounded the south jetty and headed straight for the rock. Aboard was a specially provisioned whaleboat which would be used to help make a landing, inasmuch as the derrick at the lighthouse had been destroyed, the boom shattered to splinters.

The new weather front had yet to hit, so at dawn the whaleboat was lowered with a seasoned crew at the oars, and aboard were Merrill and Asquith. A maze of ropes was extended between the tender and the whaleboat while a Lyle gun fired others to the rock. Thus, the whaleboat was the go-between while a temporary landing rig was improvised which eventually permitted a daring aerial ride to the battered station by the inspectors. They were greeted with great relief by Keeper Hill, who had already made his assessment of the damages. Merrill was appalled at the destruction. Thousands of dollars would be required to right the wrongs. The lens would have to be replaced, iron bolts unearthed from three feet in solid rock would have to be reset, iron railings flattened by huge boulders replaced, fog signal trumpets unclogged, outside fuel and water tanks, knocked askew, put back in place—plus countless other repairs.

The inspectors worked tirelessly to list all the needed items, and then before the fury of the next storm struck, made it back to the tender with no small amount of concern, the waves licking at their boat all the way. In defiance of the nasty seas, supplies were landed in canvas-covered boxes floated in on the bight of a line handled by the keepers at one end and the boat crew at the other.

Hoisting the whaleboat aboard, the *Manzanita* made knots back to the Astoria base to secure equipment for repairing the lighthouse. In the interim, the Tillamook keepers set about to fix whatever they could until needed materials arrived. As a result of their long exposure, two of their number came down with severe cases of influenza. This necessitated a special trip by the tender *Rose* to remove them to a mainland hospital. Captain Jens H. Jensen, master of the *Rose*, in addition to his crew, was accompanied by six Coast Guardsmen from Point Adams—experienced men, who succeeded in setting up the breeches buoy under the most difficult conditions. It was a risky undertaking on that Thanksgiving Day, but the rescue was accomplished despite extremely adverse weather—wind, rain, bitter cold and white-lipped combers roaring tumultuously.

Later, a working party was dispatched to the rock to make major repairs and eventually to install a new navigation light in the battered lantern room. It was not until February of 1935 that the basic job was completed. Many scars remained.

The badly damaged Fresnel lens was replaced by a Great Lakes-type aero-marine revolving beacon, electrically operated. To protect the new light, a metal mesh cage was placed around the glass panes in the lantern. Flying fragments would thereafter be catapulted back into the sea.

The hour was now late. Time had passed me by as I eagerly read the old lighthouse records, but on leaving that attic library I felt I had gained a new cross-section into life in a lighthouse, a landmark to some, a snare to others. Though the life might have seemed repetitious to the outside world, to me it was beginning to assume a reality like a story that never grows old. True, I had hated my existence for many weeks, but things suddenly took on a glow. The sea in all its moods became fascinating—the storms, the birds, the strange creatures of the deep. Long blinded to this eternal show through civilized breeding, I now had the blinders lifted from my eyes, and I praised God for his blessings.

Left: May 1935 saw the new derrick boom getting a workout. The cage being hoisted carries four men while others stand by in a lighthouse service workboat. Right: East end of the lighthouse showing stairway and tram cable, storage tanks and sacks of coal.

Tillamook Rock Light Station about 1895, with an extremely flat summer sea. The lighthouse tender *Columbine* is anchored, offloading materials for the station. Comparisons can be made when one considers the length of the vessel, which was 145 feet between perpendiculars. Note the roof of the lighthouse. The picture was taken before a second story was added.

Left: The almost legendary lighthouse keeper Bob Gerloff, who put in years of service at Tillamook Rock, would never go ashore when his turn for leave came. He had a secret love affair with the rock and worried about the light when forced to retire in the 1930s. Each evening he would go to the seawall at Seaside to be sure the light came on. Among other talents, he was an oil painter.

Below: This swarthy-looking party shows the keepers of Tillamook Light and some personnel from the lighthouse tender *Columbine* around 1900. (Gainor Minot photo)

Anyone should have marveled at the massive aquarium that surrounded me; the glowering shapes that haunted the depths, the rise and fall of the surf revealing and again effacing fringes of brown and green seaweed and clusters of vividly colored starfish, urchins, mussels and limpets, all fighting to maintain their hold against the elements. When one tired of submarine life, there were the countless numbers and varieties of sea fowl that hovered over the brawling, brutish stretch of water, punctured by reefs and rocks. Indeed this was the turning point in my lighthouse career.

To everyone, sometime in the course of his life, comes that transcendent longing to get away from it all—to retire to a lonely haven set apart from the rest of the world, perhaps a spot where long rollers crash ceaselessly against the malformed seacoast, where a vast expanse is fed by a lusty torrent springing from the green foothills beyond—virgin land, free from infernal progress. Business as usual is especially difficult for the rebel to live by.

Yes, that night as I read about the rock's early years, I remembered having once had illusions of grandeur about places set apart from the world. Little did I realize that fate would give me the role of a lighthouse keeper, not in a peaceful spot such as one might see from the deck of a pudgy ferryboat crossing a protected inlet, but on a notorious crag, commonly labeled the most treacherous of lighthouses, a weather-beaten sentinel given to the ways of the sea, streaked with salt, scarred and bruised by the ravages of time. From its portals spread the oldest and greatest of oceans, for almost half of the water of the world is in the vast Pacific, endless, dangerous, and furrowed by steep trenches.

Having hurdled the first obstacle in conquering the pangs of isolation, there was still another problem to defeat, namely, transformation of mind over matter. True, the eerie light and the vexatious foghorn were a malediction in themselves, and the varied assortment of characters who inhabited lighthouses were without precedent, but through it all I at last gained a feeling of responsibility apart from my surroundings—that of keeping the light burning for struggling seafarers.

# CHAPTER 5

# REPETITIOUS DUTY AND CULINARY MAYHEM

The fragrant aroma of coffee permeated the kitchen as we finished the noon meal. The talk, what there was of it, revolved around "boat day," which if the weather cooperated, would be on the morrow. Allik was due for his shore leave and would be replaced by the third assistant keeper. I learned from Roy that the replacement was one named Ed Stith, but beyond that everybody was reluctant to say much.

Though rains still drenched the rock, the ides of March were nearly over and spring was not far off, all of which tended to warm the cockles of my heart. The boat's arrival was always a big and exciting occasion because it meant mail and packages from home, plus a resupply of food to fill the sometimes empty shelves of the pantry. The lighthouse was anything but self-sufficient. Rain water could be taken from the roof into a cistern in time of emergency but as far as solid foods, supplies and fuel were concerned everything had to be imported. Nothing grew on the rock and though some of the keepers had at one time or another tried some plants inside, they too seemed to wither and die. Nor did animals adapt to the solid formation of the place. George told me, in one of his few talkative moods, that they once had a dog brought out by the tender, as a mascot. With no trees, grass or even a dandelion on which to lift his leg, he despaired of life, and, according to the head keeper, "just disappeared one day."

Nor had a cat fared any better—no rodents to chase—even rats and mice had abandoned the rock. The feline just up and died one day. It seemed obvious to me that animals as well as humans suffered from loneliness and privation.

I asked George why they didn't install a fake fire hydrant for the troubled canine.

He looked at me quizzically and grunted, but I couldn't help noticing the slightest hint of a grin on that otherwise stone face as he removed himself from my company.

A lesson I was fast learning, "light housekeeping," meant just that. Anything not put in its proper place was a misdemeanor. There was no place for junk in the working areas of the lighthouse nor was dust permitted to collect. I was getting housemaid's knee, and the old brass dustpan, the original from 1881, was my chief companion. I became proficient at keeping the tower area sparkling clean and the floor highly polished. It surprised me after so short a time that even though no visitors came to the lighthouse, I was showing a semblance of pride in my rock-bound home.

The lighthouse register showed that about 300 persons had visited the lighthouse since its inception and many of those were on business or repair junkets. Noticeably missing were the names of women. From the outset, the government decreed the place "a male station, far too confined for both sexes." Never in the history of the lighthouse had any woman been considered for duty, and it was to remain that way till Tillamook's last hour of service. Not that the sight of a woman, especially a pretty, well-stacked one, wouldn't have been a sight to behold during those dark, dreary, foggy intervals, but even after the Coast Guard took over the Lighthouse Service, the ban on women at Tillamook continued just as before. On one occasion shortly before I arrived on the rock, Roy told me that a SPAR (Coast Guard lady) accompanied the male inspection officer on his annual inventory and that the keepers stood around and ogled the cute little gal during the entire operation. A rosy glow came over the face of my informant as he recalled the incident.

It was then I understood that even old lighthouse keepers never grow immune to the charms of the opposite sex.

After standing the early watch, I retired but tossed through the remainder of the night anxiously awaiting the boat arrival in the morning. I even asked the good Lord to provide the proper sea conditions so the craft would not be cancelled. My request was granted as the pale dawn broke on a moderate ocean. The Pacific's trackless expanse was enhanced to the east by the coastal headlands that rose sharply from the silver breakers. I scanned the sea to the north, looking for the motor lifeboat, but it wasn't to be seen. Noon arrived and Allik, packed and ready to go, was becoming a bit anxious. George and Roy seemed little concerned but I knew the latter had ordered some books on golfing, and that always sparked his interest.

From the kitchen, I kept scanning the ocean with the glasses, at last sighting a mere speck heaving and rolling in the far distance. Sometime later, Roy entered the derrick house and George and I were on the landing platform with Allik. I took special notice of the treatment the returning keeper would be accorded on boarding the breeches buoy. No problem. He was picked off the lifeboat with precision, not even wetting his feet. The boom made its arc with relative ease and as the cable dropped slowly we stepped in to lend a hand. While struggling out of the breeches buoy, the returnee's belt snagged in the ropes and pulled his pants to his knees, long enough to reveal a sturdy pair of red underwear. We couldn't contain our laughter. Amid a volley of profanity, he yanked his britches to proper latitude and forced a half smile.

So this was Ed Stith. Eyeing him with curiosity I wondered what kind of an individual he was. I was somewhat impressed that he noticed my presence.

"Hey, something new's been added to the old crag," he bellowed. "Name's Ed," he volunteered.

As I shook his big warm hand the lines in his face seemed to tell of a somewhat troubled life. His eyes, however, were deep and understanding. He appeared as one who had been through it all, one who might listen to another's problems—and probably one familiar with Astoria bars and their barmaids. As I was soon to learn, he was a good man but one with his share of problems. He had been transferred to several district stations, yet had stuck with the work through thick and thin. No awards or trophies were on his shelves and he, like George, would never be a candidate for the best-dressed man of the year.

Bidding farewell to Allik, we watched him fly off into space. I wondered if I looked as ridiculous as he did 75 feet in the air clinging white-knuckled to the ropes, legs hanging out through the canvas pants of the life ring. From a distance he resembled a pregnant pelican.

My excitement turned to full joy when the boom swung back over us, the bulging cargo net attached to the cable hook. George was quick to inform me that the contents were not to be raided until he gave the order. A variety of items were in the net and two of us had all we could do to drag it from the platform over to the little wheeled trolley—which traveled topside on a cable activated by a small engine.

When I finally got my packages from home, plus two perfume-scented letters from girl friends, one a SPAR in Portland and the other a local in Aberdeen, I didn't even take time to watch the motor lifeboat depart. I just hurried up to my attic hideaway, and while devouring Mom's delicacies, read my love letters over and over to the strains of the well-grooved recording, "Born to Lose."

I came down out of cloud nine wishing that I was aboard the lifeboat, shore-bound. Instead, I was told that my turn to be cook had arrived. Ever since being exiled to the rock I had hoped it would never come, for I knew that by the time the keepers tasted my culinary efforts, disputes and complaints over the fog signal would no longer be the primary source of disagreement. And how right I was. The conversation increased at the table and much of it was about the food.

Ed came to the rescue, compassionate sort that he was. He gave me some hints about the old cook stove and some of his favorite recipes, and on his off time would sneak into the kitchen and lend a hand.

Those guys were big eaters. No meal was complete without meat, gravy and potatoes, plus vegetables, salad and dessert, but I had to admit that their taste buds must have dulled somewhat during my K.P. tenure. I got Ed to do some of the cooking, promising to wash the dishes for him when his turn as cook came around. That had been my specialty during a year's duty aboard an armed Coast Guard cutter based at Grays Harbor. It was the lowest job on shipboard and I was appropriately called the "pearl diver." I hadn't minded washing dishes for a crew of 50 every day, because I could always stay warm and clean when the savage North Pacific storms howled.

I'll not say more about my duties as chef but I must share a later experience when on Thanksgiving Day my turn to be cook rolled around again.

The holiday menu supplies had long before been ordered and would be delivered a day or two before Thanksgiving. On the day the boat was to arrive, weather conditions were anything but ideal. A heavy rain pelted down from black, wool-like clouds. Despite the weather we were informed by telephone that the bar was passable and that the motor lifeboat was underway.

The thought of roast turkey, like my mother made, whetted my appetite, but when I realized I would be cooking the big fowl, my enthusiasm cooled abruptly. There was quite a difference between frying a steak and producing a golden-brown bird with all the trimmings.

At last the rain stopped falling, though the wind continued to gain momentum. The lifeboat was now less than a quarter mile away and appeared to be losing headway. George went down to the derrick house to warm up the engines. When the boat was in the lee shadow of the rock, the boom was already in position and the cable threading toward its deck. Busy hands worked at either end and after the exchange of keepers, one of whom got slightly dunked, the cargo net was attached. The boat rolled so violently that every time the hookup was about to be made, the craft drifted away. When it was in the correct position, some of the supplies worked themselves out of the net. Like a dog chasing its tail, the lifeboat went round and round trying to regain the desired position.

One of my cohorts nudged me.

"Look down there. It's our turkey!" he said excitedly.

From our vantage point it looked more like a small bite than a full-sized gobbler. Precaution would be taken by the derrick op-

erator to see that the turkey didn't get the "deep six," at least that
was our hope.

On receiving the upward pointed hand, George jerked the
levers so hard the net literally flew into the air and the bird, right
at the very top, worked loose, balancing precariously. We stood
by helplessly, waiting for it to plunge into the heaving ocean.

"Goodbye turk," I heard one of the keepers say, throwing his
hands over his eyes. The other claimed that George had a shackle
bolt between his ears, but I kept thinking I might not have to cook
a turkey after all.

Then it happened. The bird dropped out of the net, and as it
was about to plummet seaward, its claw caught on the end strand
and hung there. For several long minutes it swung back and forth
like the pendulum of a clock. Moments of silence followed, but
the boom keep swinging till immediately over us. Then as the
cable threaded out, the claw gave way and the fowl dropped
into our midst. One of the keepers, not desiring turkey stew,
tried to break the fall. The bird remained pretty much intact,
perhaps only a broken bone or two.

The rescuer personally carried the fallen fowl topside, everything else being taken up to the lighthouse entrance on the
cable cart.

Next morning, scanning the pages of the lighthouse cookbook
while picking pinfeathers, I put together a ham-and-egg breakfast for the crew.

Playing the part of chef was definitely not my line of work.
Fending for myself I could manage, but cooking for a family of
lightkeepers with hollow legs was something else. My boyhood
"Friendly Indian" days had taught me a few of the rudiments of
making breakfast, though my pancakes never did come out right.
But a Thanksgiving feast, that was a different story. I hugged the
cookbook as if it was my constant companion, dashing here and
there like a punch-drunk shadow boxer on the afternoon of combat. The clatter of pots, pans and dishes resembled a Saturday
night hoedown. Occasionally the curious eyes of one of the keepers would peer in to see that all was under control. One look
should have told them that the situation at best was chaotic.

When the turkey was at last in the oven, the day was wearing on and so was I. After the bird had stewed in its juice for a few hours it was time for a "look-see." That was a mistake, for while the peep show was underway, the water in the potato pan boiled over, causing me to jump up so quickly that I upset the pan full of turkey. Gravy grease oozed out on the floor and the bird skidded through it. The gobbler was too hot to handle. I raised it a few inches but hastily dropped it. Talk about a bird with "dropsy." The last thump on the floor virtually ended its will to hang together. It was so badly mutilated that the dressing tumbled out to the tune of boiling water hissing on the top of the stove like a popcorn wagon on the Fourth of July.

Fearing my comedy of errors would bring some irate keeper to the scene, I hastily sought a towel in which to wrap the bird and get it back in the pan. There being none available, I had no alternative but to remove my T-shirt to perform the task. Though it was more than a little unorthodox, I had no choice if I didn't wish to be on the receiving end of a tongue-lashing from my cohorts. If at that moment they could have seen the battered bird, I would have eaten crow. Boy, would I have eaten crow!

Turkey, dressing, sweet potatoes, mashed potatoes, beans, salad, apple pie—the whole works were on the menu. It sounded good but the proof was in the taste and I was in no hurry to sample my efforts.

When the zero hour arrived, I hesitatingly rang the dinner bell and waited. The keepers came in one by one as though marching to their funerals, and well they might have been. Taking their regular places around the table, they sat down like monks in a monastery. Each tucked a paper towel in his shirt collar to corral evasive morsels, and then promptly began on the preliminary course, creating a chorus of gluttonous sounds.

Nary a word was spoken. It's a strong stomach that has no turning and it became evident that all three had cast-iron bread baskets.

As the grinders did their job, George finally looked up at me.

"Where's your shirt?" he demanded. " 'Tain't sanitary to cook without your shirt."

I had almost forgotten I was barechested, but wasn't about to relate the details for obvious reasons. Floundering for an answer, I finally pleaded the oppressive heat of the oven, while slowly stealing across the slippery floor to hide the evidence under a dishpan.

The displeasure of the accuser was somewhat quelled when I brought the battered bird to the table and set it in front of him to carve. The gobbler resembled a punctured football and I was fully prepared for the "fall-out." As the knife slipped through the meat, the rosy flesh hinted at a slightly underdone condition. Ironically, there were no major complaints till Roy bit into the dressing.

"What's this?" he questioned. All the time I kept thinking of dirt and hair from the floor.

"That's the sweetest stuff I ever ate," he went on.

At that juncture I remembered the salt and sugar were in similar containers, unmarked, and I had evidently used the sweetener. Ed came to the rescue.

"Put it on another plate and eat it for dessert," he quipped. "You wouldn't know the difference anyway unless it had a golf ball in it." That brought a round of laughter and an easing of tensions. The meal continued peacefully despite the fact the mashed potatoes were full of lumps, the beans stringy, sweet potatoes dry, the apple pie crust underdone, and the coffee almost muscular. There were other culinary breaches, but it seemed the keepers had waited so long for the meal, they refrained from a preponderance of criticism.

It was a comforting feeling when the last mouthful had been devoured, for I knew if they could down that meal they would eat anything. Leaving the table empty, the trio marched out the way they came in, one puffing an odoriferous cigar, another with a wad of tobacco in his jaw.

I was left alone with a picked-over turkey carcass containing several broken bones, but somehow the table full of dirty dishes didn't look so bad. The ordeal was over.

# CHAPTER 6

# HOW DID I GET HERE?

Often I pondered about my home on the rock, this upheaval from the cataclysmic past. Perhaps it was a stubborn bubble of lava broken off from a massive flow, or something belched up from under the then non-existent seabed. However it was formed, it remained a stubborn, unmovable outcast that had stood the test of great time. For most of its existence it had stood solitary, undisturbed by human beings.

When the early Indians migrated to the Northwest coast they found habitable surroundings along what would later be known as the Oregon coast. For perhaps many thousands of years, generation after generation, they had looked out toward this strange, overhanging monolith protruding from the sea. But they gave it a wide berth, not only because it appeared unapproachable but they believed it to be the abode of spirit gods. A legend told of an underwater tunnel that ran from Tillamook Head underneath the ocean up inside of Tillamook Rock, where only supernatural beings could go.

Though in their sturdy canoes, Indians fished the bountiful waters around its base, it is quite possible that no Indians landed on the rock during all those centuries. Yet here I was, "at home" on that rock.

It all began while I was at a Coast Guard station in Pacific City. In the summer, fishermen frequented the area, but for the rest of the year the place was a wind-whipped ocean-front hamlet. Sand dunes were piled up nearby, and winding around the little settlement was a sluggish river which literally crept toward the ocean.

One night a few months after World War II was declared, the station truck had taken my partner Joe and me up a glorified cow path, to begin ten miles of beach-patrol duty. With no communications along the beach, he carried a Walkie-Talkie; a patrol dog was in my charge. With a toot of the horn the truck rumbled back down the hill and we began our hike, a mile through the trees and underbrush to a bold cliff from which a narrow switchback trail led down to the beach.

The patrol dog was the cause of it all, a pointer named Pluto, a dead ringer for Disney's creation. He had no nose for sniffing out foreign agents, but he excelled at chasing birds, not knowing how to point. When no birds were around, he busied himself chasing his tail.

On that particular evening we followed the usual "illegal" procedure of unleashing the hound and letting him chase birds to his heart's content. Once free of his bonds, Pluto struck out on his own, panting, sniffing and barking up one trail and down another. When we reached the high cliff above the ocean, the dog was already there. It was a steep drop, broken only by a single shelf of sand. Suddenly Pluto paused at the cliff's edge. Down swooped a formation of sandpipers. He snapped his jaws shut; no catch! At that same moment, a breeze caught his hind quarters, lifted him up, and over he went.

We ran down the trail as fast as our feet would carry us, for we knew that regardless of Pluto's mental merit he was government property for which we were responsible. Joe pointed to a protected indentation under the cliff, where rising vertically from the sands we saw a tail and two legs spinning like a thrashing machine. The dog's fall had evidently been broken by the ledge above. Nevertheless, he was well embedded in the sand. Except for a deep gash across his forehead, Pluto appeared to be in one piece. For a few minutes he staggered about on his unsteady legs but then suddenly collapsed—alive but immobile.

Though we had the Walkie-Talkie, it was a standing order that all messages must be sent in code, and the only near equivalent signified "Patrolman Injured." Joe made contact with the station, sent the message and named a coded rendezvous spot, but could say nothing more.

We made a stretcher of rope and driftwood, draped the pooch over it and commenced the arduous patrol in the gathering dusk. After tramping along that isolated beach for a mile or two, Joe tripped over an old whiskey bottle that had drifted in on the tide. He picked it up and discovered it was a quarter full. Tired of listening to the dog's whining, he gave him a swig to put him out of his misery. One look at the aged bottle's contents suggested mighty potent stuff. The dog grimaced, gulped, and swallowed.

"He likes it!" cried Joe. "He wants more." So my partner gradually emptied the bottle into the appreciative dog, who panted and drooled, then finally fell into a deep sleep.

After three long hours of sand pounding, Joe looked at the luminous dial on his watch and announced that we were near our rendezvous. At the break in the beach we walked up to the driftwood line and sat down on a log to await the canine ambulance.

Except for the incessant pounding of the surf, the night was silent, and we were too weary to disturb the air with conversation. As the minutes ticked by with no sign of the truck, we wondered if Joe's message had been properly interpreted. Then from the distant hills came a muffled sound. We cupped our hands to our ears but instead of a pickup truck, it sounded more like a fleet of heavy-duty trucks. Suddenly Joe jumped up, insisting that he heard someone sneeze. Next came the sound of a thousand feet crunching through the soft sand.

We grabbed our rifles and stared into the impenetrable night. A cloud suddenly drifted away from the solid mass in the northern sky, just long enough to let a faint speck of moonlight peek through. Dimly outlined were the figures of a platoon of soldiers with fixed bayonets. Struck by the same impulse, we both flopped on our stomachs. Beads of sweat dampened our brows, for what was being enacted before us suggested nothing less than a full scale enemy invasion. Had the Japanese landed? Too frightened to move, we just buried our chins in the sand and prayed.

"Stand where you are; you're surrounded!" came a strident command.

Then, as the moon peeped through again, we saw an army officer step out of the darkness, holding the business end of a pistol in our direction and ordering us to come out with our hands over our heads. We did. When he was sure we were not foreign agents, he asked, "Which one is injured and where are the invaders?" The soldiers closed in, joined by familiar faces from the Coast Guard Station. Everyone waited for our answer.

"Your message, patrolman injured!" repeated the officer. "Where are the foreign agents?"

Joe pointed to the dog and attempted an explanation, a difficult task, especially because the soldiers had been aroused from warm bunks to repel what they thought was an invasion, all on account of an erroneous interpretation of our message. When the uniformed mob learned that the dog was the injured patrolman and that there were no invaders, angry passions flared. Amid frowns, snarls and growls, we handed them the stretcher bearing the indisposed hound, who woke up just long enough to hiccup.

Thereafter, having difficulties adjusting to superior officers, I wrote a letter to Coast Guard headquarters asking for "isolated duty" where there existed the least amount of gold braid. Fully expecting a lighthouse in the far northern climes of Alaska or perhaps a radar station on some remote atoll in the South Pacific, I was told a transfer was already on the way.

Ironically, I found myself attached to the Portland base as a chaplain's assistant and was then shifted to the Beaver Ammunition Dump near Clatskanie, Oregon. It was a sister military ammunition bunker to the facility at Port Chicago on San Francisco Bay. At dockside, armed merchant ships, mostly American and Russian, loaded around the clock taking on everything from bullets to 1,000-pound bombs for the war effort. Stevedore gangs worked ceaselessly in the holds, under the direction of military overseers. Coast Guard and Marine units were attached to the operation and high-ranking officers of all branches of the service came and went. Nobody got into or off the base without a special pass, and armed guards stood ready at the gate for any eventuality.

The trouble all started one night in the hold of an aged Russian cargo vessel. As an uninformed Seaman First Class, I was on guard supposedly overseeing the stevedoring effort of seasoned civilian longshoremen. Nothing more than a figurehead, I walked around in the dank, rat-infested cavities of the ship as 500-pound bombs were lowered by clattering deck winches and stowed on racks for overseas transit.

Enter one, a Coast Guard officer in charge of the Beaver contingent. A "90-day wonder," he was little versed in the proper stowage of cargo, though pretending to be an expert. Already he had me on the blacklist for an incident aboard another Russian ship where some Soviet crewmen had taken a liking to me. I had a little communication book, issued by the military, with the simplest Russian words, and during a five-day loading period, standing guard on their ship, they got their jollies out of my feeble attempts at conversing in their language. On the day before the ship departed, three crewmen insisted I stay for the midday meal. I tried to explain that this was not permitted, but was soon to learn Russians don't take no for an answer. They led me into the mess and plunked me down, rifle and all. I was amazed to find on my right side a Russian woman doctor, auburn hair, brown eyes, very attractive and quite conversive in English.

Realizing my time to be relieved of duty had arrived, I tried to depart after slurping down a weird Russian soup. But, it was not to be, for as soon as the bowl was emptied it was again filled to the brim, and when I would get up to go they would force me to sit down again. I must admit the company of the doctor was refreshing, as most of the Russian women aboard were shabbily attired, unattractive and not allowed to fraternize with outsiders.

It was almost an hour before my "niets" were accepted. Gracefully thanking my hosts, I rushed off the gangplank into the arms of the officer of the day, which meant an appearance before the C.O. My explanation of "carrying out proper international relations" bore little acceptance, and my next three liberties were cancelled.

Now, some days later, back to the other Soviet vessel. My C.O. was coming down the ladder into the hold. The stevedores had, in my estimation, done an admirable job of loading bombs on stacked wooden racks, and certainly I was not about to tell them they didn't know their business. Came the officer looking for a place to show his authority, and I happened to be in the right place at the wrong time. His voice reverberated in the hold.

"Get with it you numbskull!" I knew he was speaking to me. The longshoremen ceased work momentarily and listened.

"These bombs aren't braced properly," he informed me. Before I could open my mouth he took his foot and gave those bombs a mighty kick which started three block-busters rolling with increasing speed off the rack into the bilge. Crash! Though the activating mechanisms were not affixed, there was powder in the hold, and by instinct the stevedores dived to the half deck. Fortunately nothing ignited.

If war restrictions had not been in effect, I think the longshoremen would have strung up the officer by the thumbs, but after considerable grumbling, they returned to work to right the wrong. But not me. My big mouth, as always, got in the way. Furious at such ignorance, this maverick rendered his opinion straight from the shoulder, leaving little unsaid.

Never in my life had I seen a man more livid. He literally shook from head to toe. Every nerve in his body seemed tensed and large veins stood out on his forehead. I thought he would kill me. His pride was seriously damaged, his authority questioned.

Needless to say, the cargo operation ceased once again, the men thoroughly enjoying the incident.

The lowest rated man on the base had told off his commanding officer. Ordered topside post-haste, my duty ended early that night. My sentence was 18 hours of KP duty per day, seven days a week, six hours for sleep, during which I was restricted to the barracks, no liberty, no leave and no termination date. And as though he had nothing better to do, that C.O. personally supervised my repeated scrubbings of the floor.

After a few days of this treatment I grew very tired and resentful. The C.O. was licking his chops like a fox that had devoured a rabbit, and as long as possible he would keep on the pressure.

Then it happened. The Port Chicago Ammunition Dump blew up on July 17, 1944. Some 322 persons perished. Damage spread as far as downtown San Francisco. Two merchant ships were totally destroyed along with several smaller craft. Buildings of the facility lay in ruins. The Beaver base was immediately placed on emergency status. Would our base be next? Those fears were intensified the following day when a boxcar loaded with ammo was brought into the yard with the seal broken on its door.

The guard was tripled, and a special meeting of high-ranking officers was summoned. They were to discuss military procedure at a midday luncheon. Meantime, I was fighting my own little war, fingers worked to the bone and body weary. Enough was enough. I didn't want that kind of treatment anymore, but my timing was bad.

The C.O., after another of his infamous tongue-lashings, informed me that I would be totally responsible for seeing that all was elaborately set up for the conference, not a speck of dust anywhere. Resentment had been building up in me for days. On the night before the conference I decided to go over the hill. The Port Chicago tragedy was a stumbling block but still I was determined.

No sure way out of the reservation existed. There were guards around the perimeter of the base and at the gate. Guards also rode the trains and orders had been issued to shoot any suspicious intruders. The only possible escape route was by walking the rails, which at best was risky. At the end of my 18-hour grind I returned to the barracks. Just after midnight while the others were fast asleep, I packed a few items, stuffed my sleeping bag under the covers and then stole out into the dark of night. Making my way through the scrub brush behind the barracks without benefit of a flashlight, I stumbled toward the rails, a good quarter mile away. Just as I reached the tracks, a locomotive near the dump area started up, its probing headlight illuminating the rails. Terrified, I did an immediate backward flip into a chasm below the railbed. I lay motionless, my heart beating like a trip-hammer. Surely they must have seen me. Remaining motionless as the engine rolled by, I could see, in silhouette, guards hanging to the side with fixed bayonets.

On gaining my composure, I crept through the thickets below the rails, gathering my share of scratches from berry vines, but the darkness made progress slow. On nearing the boundary of the base, I took one of the big risks of my life. Using the railroad ties for a path, I began running at full speed and didn't slow my pace for almost three miles, hoping I wouldn't be sighted. When I finally reached the highway, it was 3 a.m., and very cold. My destination was Portland, where "Smitty," a carrot-topped Coast Guard Spar was stationed. I had met her during my duty in Portland and knew she would help me.

Certain that my escape had not yet been discovered, I began hitchhiking. Few cars were traveling the road at that hour but to my surprise one of them stopped and picked me up. In Portland, I got myself a bite to eat and an inexpensive hotel room. After a few hours of rest I put a call through to Smitty, who promptly urged me to turn myself in. I agreed to meet her and talk it over but was determined to enjoy a few days of freedom before facing the consequences. She agreed to keep me notified of news involving my escape, and she didn't have to wait long.

The C.O. at the Beaver site had barged into the barracks that morning when informed I had not reported for duty. Infuriated, he kicked my bunk and pulled the blanket back. On seeing a stuffed seabag, his temper flared and in short order the word was out for all MP's in the district to be on the lookout. I was charged with dereliction of duty, going over the hill, insubordination and several other counts. I became Coast Guard public enemy number one.

Zero hour came a few days later. The hearing room was austere. I was taken in and seated well ahead of the proceedings. All I could think of was a dishonorable discharge, a jail sentence, loss of voting rights, denial of citizenship, etc., but most of all I feared the effect it would have on my parents, who had always looked on me as a law-abiding young man.

The minutes ticked slowly by and I was still alone. The hour of the hearing came and went. Another hour passed. I twisted, turned and fussed, when suddenly the commanding officer of the base, a career Coast Guard captain—a large hulk of a man— entered the room unescorted. Immediately he gave me a dressing down, the like of which I had never before received. He let me have it with both barrels. I took it all in silence. Then came the shocker.

"I never want to see your face around here again. Pick up your transfer papers on the way out." The hearing was never convened, no mark was made against my name, nor did I ever again see the C.O.'s of either station. Ironically, my transfer was to a seagoing Coast Guard cutter.

So the second stepping stone on the road to Tillamook was laid, and after a rather checkered career aboard the cutter *Nemaha*, new orders came through with the notation:

"Isolated duty. Report immediately to Point Adams Coast Guard Station for transfer to Tillamook Rock Light Station."

Playing a game of seagull rugby. One gets the fish and the others try to take it away. Note the gull in the left foreground scooping up the fish while in flight. (Dennis C. Mavity photo)

# CHAPTER 7

## CAMPING OUT AND GREEN APPLES

Three months of continuous duty on an isolated crag had seemed a long time. Now at last I had been granted a slight reprieve from my rocky hermitage. The restricted quarters made me think how wonderful it would be to walk a mile in a straight line or to see a variety of faces instead of the familiar three. Even more thrilling was the thought of seeing members of the opposite sex, for on the rock, it was easy to forget that half of the world's population constituted the feminine sex.

How excited I was on reaching the boat! That voyage northward from the rock along the coastal rim and across the Columbia bar is only about 25 miles, but what a 25-mile trip it can be. Probably no small stretch of ocean has a more evil reputation for roughness. Many times when the Pacific winds lashed the sea and the tide-rips and cross-currents swirled off the Columbia, those aboard the stout lifeboat desired the quiet refuge of a harbor, but there were no detours en route.

Once in the boat, a single glance told me that the same grizzled crew that had delivered me was now taking me away. Walking aft and jumping into the well, I was conscious of several pairs of eyes centering on me as if I were something that had escaped from a sideshow.

"He still looks sane," reasoned one of the crew.

"I'm not so sure!" ventured another, scrutinizing me closely. "His eyes look glassy."

"Let's see how he talks," said the third. "Gibberish, I'll bet."

I made a vain attempt to tell my inquisitors that I had not gone off my rocker and told them to save the examination until we reached shore.

"Napoleon orders his ship from exile," jested the boatswain. "Prepare to drop off the royal lines."

The engine throbbed as we got underway. The helmsman jockeyed the craft skillfully and the others became too absorbed with their duties to play Napoleon any longer for fear of meeting their Waterloo. As the boat gathered headway, I glanced astern and waved to the keepers, who looked like ants on a great ant hill. Soon the pyramid of basalt diminished like a melting ice cube as a thickening drizzle closed in about us. I was homeward bound.

Then came my visit home, up Seattle way. Ah, yes, home sweet home. At least I thought so until word got around that I was a lighthouse keeper. For several days I was a target for witless jests such as: "Well, son, it must be pretty soft living off the government—no expenses at all" or, "Bet you went swimming every day, huh?"

Then there were those enjoyable hours, like raiding a food-packed refrigerator; midnight snacks deluxe. And, of course, there were females, those lovable creatures in skirts, plus all kinds and varieties of people, among whom were no lighthouse keepers. Never had I thought that standing on a busy street corner just watching people pass by could be so interesting. Many thoughts concerning my months of solitude spun wildly in my brain as I tasted once again the domesticated side of life. However, though everything was exciting, I found myself thinking that some of the frustrated population should have an assignment similar to mine, especially those concerned only with the material aspects of living, completely oblivious, as I once had been, to the abundant gifts of nature and the mighty voice of God in the wind, the rain, and the sea.

My few days of freedom were on the wane seemingly before they had begun, and in spite of my efforts to hold back time, I soon found myself atop the rock once again, back with my cell mates for another lengthy stretch—the same beetling crag and that familiar smell of the turbulent waters. For sure, there was no

gainsaying that the rock was the nastiest chunk of rubble anywhere. On the other hand, I imagined that there must be many
more undesirable places in the world—but to the newcomer who
had no understanding of the place, it could indeed seem like the
"end" of the world.

Like green timber cut and exposed to the weather, I felt considerably more seasoned for my second term. No more weeks of
torment, melancholy and dissolution, for I was now well aware
that the happiest lighthouse keepers were those who kept their
minds well occupied. My resolution was to make the most of my
months of isolation. How about pretending the place was a recreational haven? After all, the weather was looking up. Or, what
about sleeping outside with the sky for a ceiling? The latter
sounded great, so I decided to try it. Why? I was never quite sure,
for it has often been said that outdoor sleeping is the most over-
rated sport in the world. But this was different—sleeping above
the sea with a lighthouse for a bedstead and a gentle breeze waft-
ing over the rock.

Upon recalling that experience, I speak on the subject with
considerable more feeling, as I now understand why sleeping in a
genuine bed under a solid roof is sufferable to mankind. There are
various categories of sleeping out, the most common being a night
among the forested wilds, complete with insects, screams of wild
beasts, and sharp rocks puncturing the backbone. Then there are
the mountain climbers who gain such altitudes that insects refuse
to grow, leaving just a springless formation of hard rock to comfort the individual, aided only in his desire for sleep by the near
exhaustion of the day's climb. Beach sleeping and desert sleeping
have one thing in common—the sand gets so lonesome that it
crawls and sifts its way into the sleeping bag, works its way into
the pajamas, and nestles comfortably against the bare skin. I had
tested the sleeping-out fad in primitive surroundings, but sleeping
outside a lighthouse held much more promise of enjoyment—at
least so I thought.

Equipment for this little experiment consisted of a navy hammock and two blankets, nothing more. The hammock was strung
up between a ringbolt in the side of the lighthouse and a stan-

chion in the railing. The result was supposed to be simple comfort, as the breeze wafted me back and forth to the tune of the roaring sea and a sky full of stars. But what is supposed to be, and what is, are often two different things.

I was careful to pick a night when I would not be awakened for duty, plus one with ideal atmospheric conditions. At four bells on that chosen night, I gave a heavy yawn, bade the keepers goodnight, and prepared to hit the hammock for the most restful rendezvous of my life. Slipping under the blankets out of the refreshing but definitely chilly night air, I had the feeling of being a nature boy under that dazzling eternity above—a fabulous myriad of stars crisscrossed by an occasional heavenly body which left trails of red, yellow or blue. It was pleasant for a while, but the night grew infinitely colder, and from the steep cliff below, a whistling updraft surged, turning my back to ice. After a short, dark and uneventful round trip through the lighthouse to secure another blanket, I started all over again.

Now, according to the code of etiquette of the insect world, mosquitoes should only frequent hot, arid and swampy areas, but I made the startling discovery of a hardier variety which packed the wallop of a home-run king, and raised bumps the size of a pitcher's mound. I played a little game called "pull the covers over my head and come out only on near suffocation," but I was always the loser. One of those buzzing bruisers was always awaiting me on the outbound journey.

First on my back, then on my stomach; the blankets became punctuated with air holes that ventilated my bare skin with frigid air. This eventually resulted in my doing setting-up exercises at the midnight hour to keep from freezing to death. After wrestling with my hammock for another hour, I had the frightening sensation of standing on my head. Heart-palpitating fear of being dumped into the sea brought me up with a start. That fear proved to be more than imagination for the hammock ropes in back of my head had slipped and I was cradled like a log at the top of a shoot.

Readjustments made, I forced myself to take a deep sigh of relief, and an extra puff to reassure myself that it was still invigorating air that I was breathing. Climbing back into the hammock for the tenth time, I counted sheep until they grew lame and could no longer clear the top barrier. It grew even colder and, of necessity, I forgot about leaping sheep and started counting jumping blocks of ice instead, curled up in a ball for the sake of preservation. Such positions were not designed for hammocks and I was soon aware of my definite overhang. To quell my frustrations, I thought of the insects slaughtered since my siesta began. I, their foe, had been a vulnerable target, and though on the wounded list, was still on the battlefield. Then came the birds.

Sea birds supposedly rise with the first rays of dawn, but I made the shocking discovery that they remain up all night trying to outscreech one another. The powerful beam of light which revolved above my head was also a distracting feature. It gave one a spinning feeling like the ball on a roulette wheel must experience. To offset my bewilderment, I recited the alphabet backwards fifty times; counted fish jumping over the ladder to the phenomenal figure of 624; counted black spots before my eyes and finally attempted to hypnotize myself, only to roll over and discover myself wider awake than when I had started.

By three in the morning, the stars got tired and plunged into rolling clouds and the wind decided to test its lungs. Absolutely and completely miserable, I had been rewarded with not so much as a wink of sleep. Only one thing kept me in my hammock—a desire to prove to the keepers that it was great fun, especially after playing it up as short of sensational.

But the worst was yet to come, for upstairs in those black clouds, where, I could not tell, a flock of night-traveling birds was wending its way northward. Maybe it was the light that excited them, or maybe it was a roughage diet, but several of them got the same idea at the same moment and decided to get in a little target practice over the rock. Unfortunately, I was at the place in my hammock calisthenics where my head was exposed. There was absolutely no chance to take refuge. Those sky devils were hit-and-run flyers. Their ammunition struck to port, to starboard, and squarely on target, the target being my head. My resulting words have been necessarily omitted.

What made me go back for one last attempt, I shall never know, but after a hike to the wash tub for a Lava soaping of head and face, it seemed as though a climax must have been reached.

It was exactly 3:52 a.m. when I crawled under the blankets for the last time. When I was almost asleep from absolute fatigue, a scream stood my hair on end. As I jerked up like the broken main spring of a watch, the hammock flipped over, depositing me on the hardest slab this side of a morgue. Ed's dimly outlined figure stood above me, frozen in its tracks.

He had forgotten about my sleeping out, and while skirting the lighthouse on his watch, he bumped into my hammock and thought a ghost had come to claim him.

That did it! Swallowing my pride, I cut down the hammock, threw the blankets over my shoulders and re-established boarding under a solid roof. True, it did not hold the suspense, excitement and recreational possibilities of outdoor sleeping, but I am now convinced that night is for slumber and not to set an endurance record or to declare war on opposing forces of nature.

A brief lesson on how to cure an ill was learned the next day. Having overindulged in eating some green apples snitched from the pantry, a problem resulted. Suffering from the "Green Apple Two-step," the call was urgent. I ran to the bathroom, only to find it occupied by one of the keepers who had a reputation for long sittings. No other alternative remained but to make a dash for the original 1881 "Chic Sales" privy that clung on the precipice of the rock like a limpet, 90 feet directly over the ocean. The wind was howling but I dashed inside and plunged myself down. A 40-mile-an-hour whirlwind updraft erupted, virtually lifting me off the hole. That whirling dervish was like nothing I'd ever before felt on my hind side, nor ever hope to feel again. For reasons unknown, my problem ended and the urge was gone— however, I would certainly not recommend such a cure for the family medical book. I get a shaky feeling every time someone mentions the word, wind-tunnel.

Another item of intrigue at the lighthouse that frequently caught my attention was a complete rack of signal flags stowed in individual wooden niches on the engine room wall. The flags were to be used in times of emergency, but for the most part had probably remained neatly rolled since the inception of the lighthouse. On removing and unraveling some of them, great rolls of dust flew and several moths took flight.

I wondered how long since they had been used or just how effective they were. Inasmuch as the steamer lane was considerably farther west of the lighthouse than in former days, I questioned whether a ship could even see flying signal flags. Finding an 1890 *List of Merchant Vessels* in the archives, which contained a color plate of signal flag messages, I determined to find out if they were still valid. My chance came two days later when a tug towing the old wooden steam schooner *Bandon* passed within a half mile of the rock.

To catch the attention of those on the two vessels I chose a message with an impact—P flag (blue with white center) over a C pennant (white with red circle). The message it related was: "Mutiny! Want assistance!"

What I didn't know was that the signal codes for 1890 were not the same as in 1915. Still, somebody on the steam schooner must have either had a good sense of humor, or availability to a comparable signal code book of ancient vintage.

Certain that none of the other keepers were about, I took down the American flag and ran up the signal flags just as the tug and tow were abreast of the lighthouse. The ocean was calm, with just enough breeze to flutter the bunting. The signal would certainly be seen. I fully expected the vessels to stand off the rock where I could explain that it was just a joke or a hoax, but the tow continued to the northwest. I had the glasses trained in their direction and grew extremely disappointed that my efforts had gone for naught. Then, suddenly, I saw a form on the steam schooner moving toward the halyard with flags in hand. Up they went, M flag (blue with white X) over S flag (white with blue center).

Quickly I thumbed the pages of my signal bible. The answer: "Do the best you can for yourselves; no assistance can be given!" As the vessel faded into the horizon, I was certain I had detected a cynical smile on the face of the signaller. Slowly I put my "toys" back in their proper racks. Undoubtedly, there they remained, undisturbed, until the lighthouse closed down.

The magic of the shoreline as seen atop the rock, from the Columbia River bar to the lofty heights of Tillamook Head, and on southward to Mt. Neah-Kah-Nie, was a coastal sweep that had captured my imagination from the day I first arrived. This outer rim of mainland U.S.A., the western boundary of Clatsop and Tillamook counties, was especially captivating when viewed from the seaward side.

For hours I would scan the beaches through the binoculars, trying to envision how it must have appeared back in the days when only the Northwest Indians roamed about. Before the white man came, only a few tiny camps existed—no resort settlements like Seaside, Cannon Beach and Manzanita. Much of the tall timber was now gone, but the bold, rocky sentinels and stretches of sandy beach remained just as they had been for countless thousands of years, a delight to the beholder.

Mystery and intrigue revolved around tales of prehistoric shipwrecks, buried treasure, the infusion of foreign blood among the Indians, discovery of beeswax and gold and silver artifacts; swarthy pirates, marked rocks, and skeletal remains. Numerous legends handed down from one generation to the next were supported by just enough remaining evidence to keep the imagination stirred.

Oftentimes around the kitchen table I spoke with my fellow keepers about the ancient tales centering on the northwestern coast of Oregon. The rock seemed to be the hidden key, witness to the forgotten past, but this old bastion's voice was silent, and one could only draw his own conclusions.

The Kuroshio or Japanese Current, for centuries, had carried flotsam and jetsam from Oriental waters to northwest shores, including many disabled Japanese, Taiwanese and Chinese junks that were undoubtedly cast ashore, and their survivors, if any, taken as slaves. This warm ocean current sweeping past Tillamook Rock is a northward-flowing branch of the North Equatorial Current, running east of Formosa and the Japanese archipelago. Near latitude 35° N. it divides; the east branch nears the Hawaiian Islands and the North branch skirts the Asian coast, merging with cold Oyashio current.

Since 1919, the colorful Japanese glass fish floats have been found along northwest shores, having drifted thousands of miles across the Pacific after breaking loose from fishnets. We frequently saw basketball-sized floats drift past the rock like solidified ocean bubbles. Castaway Orientals who found themselves captives of prehistoric Indians left a legacy of Japanese words among the natives, which were recognized by the early explorers.

In like fashion, Spanish castaways also fell among the early Indian tribes. Shipwrecks before discovery days are known to have occurred just south of the Columbia River, on Nehalem beaches and at the entrance to the Salmon River in Lincoln County. On Nehalem Spit, some 400 tons of Ghedda beeswax—also called East Indian wax—has been uncovered through the years. Chunks of the substance were presented to Lewis and Clark, giving credence to the wreck of one or more galleons and caravels in the area.

A treasure yet to be found remains hidden on the lower slopes of Neah-Kah-Nie; marked rocks found through the years reputedly offer the key to its location. Thousands have dug but none have been rewarded with anything save sweat and toil. Teak ship timbers, bones of murdered Caucasians, as well as coins, tools and weapons of foreign make were found among the native tribes when the early discoverers and settlers came.

George and Roy had often spoken of where the treasure of Neah-kah-Nie might be hidden, and both had made tongue-in-cheek plans to search someday. On the strength of their intelligence, I made a run down the coast at a later date and was rewarded by finding a four-inch piece of the storied beeswax on a Nehalem beach. It was nothing like the great chunk in the Tillamook City museum, or the huge pieces that have been discovered by others, but it was enough to whet my appetite for treasure—most of which dwelled in the coffers of my mind.

Some say intrigue is what dreams are made of, and nothing so stirs the imagination as legends of buried treasure—jewels, pieces of eight and bullion. Would that I might have gone back in time, but alas, there I was, stuck on a rock.

Monstrous waves thunder and hiss in this spectacular assault on England's North Pier Lighthouse. Such waves, seldom caught in a photograph, attack Tillamook Rock Lighthouse when the conditions of wind and sea are right. (H.S. Thorne photo)

# CHAPTER 8

# STORMS AND THINGS

All that night it blew terribly hard, raising angered and lunging seas such as I could not remember. During my graveyard watch, the wind veered but a few points, each time slipping back on course, only to blow harder, as though it had gone out of its way to catch an extra breath. The glass was low, and though I knew greater hurricanes had hit the rock, to me it was a sight to behold. Longfellow's words rang in my ears.

> The startled waves leap over it: the storm
> Smites it with all the scourges of the rain,
> And steadily against its solid form
> Press the great shoulders of the hurricane.

The lighthouse groaned like a live creature in the mire of doom. The seas slammed against it with such shocks that I thought it would be torn from its roots and tossed into the ocean. Tons of water swept over the top of the dwelling, bringing fragments of rock and debris which were deposited with resounding concussions. The derrick boom shuddered violently and its supporting timbers appeared as if they would break loose. The jaws of the erroneously named Pacific were wide open as if waiting for its deep troughs to be fed.

As I watched the fury of the gale from behind bolted doors, I remembered having once read something about the silence of the sea—that the loud noises a man hears are not from the sea itself, not even from the gale, but from the battle between the wind and what it encounters. The rocks, reefs, capes and headlands are the sounding things. The bastions that stand against the tempest and the ships that sail it are clashing cymbals. The sailor remembers the creaking of his ship—the swinging lanterns, the loose rigging, the blocks and the billowing canvas. The beachcomber remembers the crash of the breakers as they roll ceaselessly over the endless acres of sand; and the lighthouse keeper is mindful of the cannon shot of the malignant sea hammering away at a rocky promontory. Those things form limits and bonds for the sea, but the ocean in itself is not a noisy creature. How strange and solemn it would be to view a raging sea and yet not hear a sound.

As I looked out across that battleground of nature, it seemed as though every shore on the globe must be a theater of conquest where the warlike forces of sea and land constantly opposed one another. Always packing the offensive punch, the ocean battered the staunch coastal defenders which refused to fly the flag of truce. Our sentinel, crowned with its watchtower, was like an angel of mercy in no man's land, taking the brunt of the big guns of the ocean's front-line regiments.

When I awakened the following morning, the gale had not abated an iota of its violence. Looking out the porthole of my room gave me the sensation of being in a submarine, ten fathoms down. The irascible sea had no clemency for the rock, slaughtering the southwest corner relentlessly. The breakers were all wrinkled and twisted about their crests, where the wind caught them and tossed their manes of spray into the glowering hollows behind them. Up they reared slowly, toppling over in reeling curves and breaking in dull, muffled explosions which sounded like distant charges of dynamite.

The driving winds of the storm, which had now surpassed hurricane velocity, had the salt-bitten keepers worried. Below the canopy of dirty gray cloud, the sea mounted up in great graybacks, and foam slid down their long slopes, bubbling, hissing. I heard George mumble under his breath that it was like the blow of a few years back which ripped the light out of the tower. He wore a rigid expression, as though momentarily expecting to hear gushing torrents of water charging unmolested through the lighthouse.

The structure trembled as the breakers discharged their violence at a height equal to a ten-story building. A seismograph would have shaken itself apart recording the fluctuating motions. The wire cable net around the top of the tower was warding off heavy fragments of rock, but two panes of glass had been cracked despite its protection.

This was my first genuine initiation to a full gale aboard the rock, and you haven't really lived until spending a night at the lighthouse under such conditions. You didn't dare step outside for fear of your life. Seas were not only breaching the rock but were sending green brine entirely over the lantern. Cascading water crashed to the roof of the dwelling and fog signal building. Roy told me he believed a fault in the rock existed under the kitchen and was certain someday the building would crack—a piece of intelligence that was not music to my ears.

Though the storm's fury was frightening, it was also exciting. The size and height of those waves barrelling into the fissure and sending up exploding geysers had been topics of conversation from the earliest days. Though we could feel the impact and watch the onrush of water, I had never seen a photo that could reflect the full impact. To capture the scene from an outside vantage point was a suicidal effort. Roy and Ed had once tried and narrowly escaped with their lives, having only a drowned camera to show for their efforts.

Ships never ventured near the rock under full gale conditions and if a person tried to catch the action from inside the tower, the photo resulted in a big blob of white, splattering foam.

Though fully assured that the great stone blocks of the structure would repulse the onslaught as they had for decades, the shaking of the building made one wonder about the fallibility of man's works compared to nature's anger. Someday, sometime, this bastion-like structure would succumb. The beating it took each year would have leveled most staunch buildings long before. The seas had already hammered hundreds of tons of basalt from the rock since the lighthouse was built, and it was certain that it would claim considerably more until only the hardest cores remained.

Venturing up the spiral staircase that night was even more spooky than the times the ghost had whispered its strange chant, but in the lantern house when the brine hit the window panes like rattling gravel, I automatically backed away. The wire cage fitted around the outside of the lantern house fended off the debris which went crashing back into the sea or landed on the structure roof and walkway. Sometimes, small pieces got through the net to leave their scars.

On asking the keepers how high they thought the geysers of sea water would erupt in a full gale, they estimated 160 feet, if the blow was from the southwest. It was from that direction that the seas built to mighty pyramidal acclivities before entering the fissure and going into a mad frenzy on striking the dead end.

I had seen photos of seas enveloping Minots Lighthouse off the New England coast and of Wolf Rock Light off the perilous English coast, but the Pacific coast's two most exposed lighthouses's— Tillamook and St. George Reef off the northern California coast —were seldom photographed when the nightmare seas exploded.

Great storms arouse horizontal avalanches of water, which can place in mortal danger the world's largest vessels. Annually, ships vanish from the face of the sea. An eyewitness account states that the 81,237-ton *Queen Mary*, despite her 1,000-foot length, came within inches of foundering while serving as a troop transport. She was in a severe North Atlantic gale 700 miles off the English Coast. According to the *Daily Mail*, "She listed until her upper decks were awash and those who had sailed in her since she first took to sea (1936) were convinced she would never right herself. Her safety depended on no more than five degrees. Had she gone those inches to port, the *Queen Mary* would have been no more." The shocking afterthought: she was carrying 15,000 U.S. troops to Europe, all of whom would undoubtedly have perished.

According to the Smithsonian, non-seismic waves have often reached over 100 feet in height, but on hitting a shallow shelf or obstruction they can attain tremendous heights such as at the Trinidad Head Light Station in northern California, when a blockbuster leaped up the cliff some 198 feet to the base of the lighthouse, December 28, 1914.

In the most severe sea conditions, with all the right factors, giant waves piling up on top of one another could theoretically reach a maximum of 198 feet in open ocean, though no such wave has yet been officially recorded. One logical place might be in the Gulf of Alaska. And, what terror could strike one watching a titanic wall of greenish-black liquid as tall as a giant building, rushing, tumbling, cascading toward a target 50 miles an hour, peaking to a pyramid, then crashing with the power of a million dynamos. But I was on Tillamook Rock and the eruptions of water there were the fiercest I cared to see.

I went over to check the glass again and saw something I had never before seen. The pressure was so great when a massive wall of water passed over the structure that the barometer needle actually dropped from 28.50 to 27 inches of pressure for a brief second and then shot back to the original position. This night was an adventure I wouldn't soon forget, but there was more to come.

About 3 a.m., the wind took a brief interlude. I was leaning backward in a chair near the stove to catch some warmth. Suddenly there was a bolt of thunder, the loudest I had ever heard, like a cannon fired in the room. At the very same instant, lightning flashed with dazzling brilliance. It struck the rod on the ball atop the lantern, traveled down the copper tubes to the kitchen and sent out a terrifying tongue of bluish-white which terminated less than a foot from where I was sitting. Over went the chair, my head hitting the stove. Lying there prostrate and terrified, I was unharmed except for a goose egg on my head.

Prior to that moment there had been no hint of an electrical storm. Its epicenter must have been directly over the tower and our lightning rod had not been grounded. Needless to say, we soon took care of that.

A new weather front then came in with all the fury of the first. It was a long night but certainly not a dull one.

As the storm began to blow itself out, three of us talking in the kitchen heard a loud cracking sound. Peering out through the kitchen window we noted that the flagpole at the northwest corner had been sheered off and splintered into kindling. Half of it, balancing on the railing, was soon carried over the precipice.

It was two more days before the gale warnings were lifted, allowing us to venture outside to inspect the pranks of the storm. The mountainous swells had finally lost mastery of the situation, and the leaden sky was displaying broken patches. The rock was streaked with lines of salt, left to dry by the rampaging breakers. Fragments of many descriptions were spread about everywhere and the storehouse and derrick house were flooded with seawater and kelp. What saddened me above all else, however, were the dead sea birds polka-dotting the walkway, the roof, and the level stretches of rock—a virtual cemetery of feathered fowl.

It is common knowledge that flashing lights tend to baffle birds in flight. Sometimes they flew directly into the powerful beam in the calmest of weather, but more frequently it was the stress of storms that claimed the greatest number. It is generally believed that they are blinded, but there are several recorded incidents of birds circling lighthouses on clear, windless nights for hours at a time. Then, for no apparent reason, they will dive at the light as if drawn by a magnet, attacking like a dive-bomber and shattering themselves against the panes of glass. Birds have also been observed leaving formations singly, dropping several hundred feet, then attacking a revolving beam.

Ornithologists are confused by the behavior of birds around a beam of light because their actions follow no set pattern. None of the elements of weather seem to hold the key. To say that the light infuriates birds in flight cannot be borne out, as some fold their wings and crash the light in a horizontal dive while others flutter about the light and fly away again. Birds have been studied under similar weather conditions over the same lighthouse. One time they will be completely oblivious to the beam; the next time they will attack.

As I looked over the crop of dead birds before tossing them into the sea, I recognized murres, cormorants, petrels, gulls and others I could not identify. I was later to learn from Audubon's book of a species of seabird that was observed on a singular occasion at Tillamook Rock:

The only Oregon record of the Man-o'-War [Frigatebird] bird is of the one that appeared at Tillamook Rock Light, which is located on a tiny rock just off the coast of Clatsop county. The bird was first noticed soaring over the rock on the morning of February 18, 1935. It swung slowly from side to side until sundown, when after several attempts to find a roosting place it settled on a small iron tripod. During the night it moved and the keeper on watch noticed it perched on a cable. In the morning it was found dead. Realizing that it was a stranger, Mr. Hugo Hansen (keeper) skinned it out and later presented the bird to Jewett.

Scissor-tailed, the frigatebird, whose body weighs only about five pounds, has a wing spread of seven or eight feet. Though a seabird, it does not swim but often perches on rocks in the sea or on shore. It soars like an eagle. In breeding season the male's red pouch puffs up like a balloon. It usually breeds in the West Indies, Bahamas, off the Venezuelan coast or on the islands abutting Mexico's west coast. It winters in adjacent seas of Florida, Louisiana and California. The graceful frigatebird has long been associated with ancient tales of the sea.

How this one straggler managed to get so far north is open to speculation, but it proved to be his port of no return.

There were many other occasions during my tenure of duty when birds, apparently blinded by the revolving beacon, crashed into the tower and fell to the platform. Never did I become oblivious to this tragedy that has plagued lighthouses for ages, with seemingly no solution.

# CHAPTER 9

## OBLIGATIONS AND FRUSTRATIONS

As the days moderated, rays of warm sunshine filtered through the clouds and shone upon our weather-beaten domain. With the milder weather came cleanup chores, the priority task being the painting of the lighthouse. It was rough, grooved stone, the kind that took five swings of the brush to cover a square inch, and just why it had to be painted was a moot question. Women were forbidden from the rock, visitors were not welcome, and lighthouse inspectors bypassed it on the slightest excuse.

All this, however, did not alter the fact that the lighthouse had to be painted, and on the first genuine summer day, the keepers began mixing a barrel full of white paint. Ed bemoaned the fact that he had returned in time for the annual chore almost as much as Roy was overjoyed on getting away.

It was a crisp morning with a sea as smooth as molasses. The sun had brushed the nebula aside and was doing its best to offer more than the usual token of warmth. The swells ran in long, oily folds, reflecting the clouds in distorted smudges of white and silver.

When the paint had reached a satin smoothness, George dipped several buckets into the barrel and lined them up in front of the storehouse.

"This one's yours," he informed me. "Grab a brush and ladder and start on the upper sou'west corner."

Gathering my materials, I took up my post, but after a few minutes on the ladder the sun's glare became so severe that pink spots were mirrored before my eyes. A bright sunshine, a glaring ocean and a white lighthouse were an impossible situation for naked eyes. So I sought out the headkeeper for a solution.

From a few thousand feet in the air, one sees Tillamook Rock, a little obstruction known as Half Mile Rock, and the outcrops of Tillamook Head. (E.A. Delanty photo)

Zeroing in on the rock by plane, looking directly at the western exposure. Through the years most of the windows had to be cemented over to prevent constant smashings. In some cases, portholes were set deep in the walls. One can see here the way the seas break between the two summits. The fog signal building is nearest to camera.

"I plum' forgot to tell yah about that glare," admitted George. "Easy to go blind from it. Grab that pair of colored glasses. And while we're on the subject, there's somethin' else I ain't told yah about."

"What's that?" I asked curiously.

"Them pesky kelp flies," he warned. "Maybe yah ain't seen 'em yet. They only come out on the hottest days, and this has the earmarks of the first hot day of the year. Watch out!"

"Kelp flies?"

"Yah, kelp flies, thousands of 'em. They'll drive yah down the hatch and under the bilge boards."

I thought George was pulling my leg, for I had not seen one fly of any description since coming to the rock. But there was much to learn. Shortly after I reached the top rung of the ladder, paintbrush in hand, something crawled across the back of my neck. Even after shaking my head, that something refused to budge. (My situation on a rickety ladder high above a narrow concrete walkway, with the ocean some 90 feet below, held my actions to a minimum.) Whatever it was, it finally left my neck of its own account, but it must have been a scout returning to alert the army, for within an hour the white blocks of the lighthouse, the ladder, and this painter were lined with pesky little flies. Somewhat smaller and more streamlined than a common housefly, they were three times as aggressive and quicker than streaked lightning.

Every time I swatted one it was five feet in the air before the brush landed. I continued painting, pretending to be oblivious to the intruders. That was sheer folly, for soon they were crawling on my neck, in my hair, and on my face. Some crawled over my glasses, down the inside of the lenses and into my eyes, giving me the feeling of a honeycomb swarming with insects. Wiggling, shaking and shimmying proved useless, for they continued using me like Grand Central Station until, to keep from going mad, I had to come down from the ladder where I could use all available facilities to fight them off.

Once again I sought out George and asked him how anyone could paint a lighthouse with flies crawling all over him.

"Always been a problem," he confessed. "Damn annoyin' at times, but yah got to put up with it. Fact is you're the only one paintin' in the sun. Too bad, no more shady corners. Flies ain't so bad there."

"Then why don't I wait until it gets shadier?" I suggested.

"We don't get much good weather. Gotta paint while we have the chance. Tell yah what; go get the Flit gun, spray around the area where you're paintin', cover your face, go back and try again."

I agreed to give it another whirl. On the outbound trip, loaded down with gear, I looked more like a Fuller Brush Man than a lighthouse painter. On reaching the top of the ladder it was a question as to how I could paint and manage the extra equipment at the same time. Requirements were ten easy lessons in juggling and the arms of an octopus. The act began by my putting the paintbrush under one armpit, the bucket in the fold of the other arm, the paint rag in my mouth. Then I had two legs to straddle the ladder and two hands with which to pump the spray gun. After a thorough saturation with insecticide, I reversed the procedure by shifting the paint rag to my right back pocket, the Flit gun to the left back pocket, the paintbrush to one hand and the bucket to the other.

Now all seemed ready—but I had forgotten to cover my head and neck. Then the eternal triangle continued—switch the paint bucket back to the bend of my left arm, place the brush under my chin, hang onto the ladder with one hand and with the other pull the sweater over my head.

Everything went well for almost ten minutes when a scout fly returned to test the tender meat around my waist, laid bare by pulling my sweater over my head. Another wiggle and a jerk were wasted effort. It was as if a box of sugar had been opened, for flies were soon pouring in the opening, fanning out in all directions under my shirt. It was absolute torment.

After two hours, distractions had made my progress noticeably slow. Then came the crowning setback. Those heartless unmentionables crawled up inside my pants, concentrating on tickling the hairs of my legs until I was forced into a balancing feat that would have eclipsed Barnum & Bailey's best. Before it was over, the bucket of paint flipped out of my hand, smearing white paint all the way down to the ocean. It was then that I went on a sit-down strike, refusing to paint another block unless given equal rights with the other keepers—for they had it all planned that I should paint the fly-infested hot spots. When I protested they claimed seniority rights, but we worked out a compromise and my task was eased a trifle.

The episodes of the ensuing days were somewhat repetitious, and needless to say, it was a time of jubilation when the lighthouse gleamed under its new coat of white, set off by a jet-black lantern. Smeared with paint from head to toe, eyes bloodshot, and muscles sore, I considered myself a tried and tired painter, and would highly recommend a similar apprenticeship for one who wished to learn painting the hard way.

Another week slipped by before the last of the paint disappeared from under my fingernails. It was a quiet Sunday afternoon, almost as if the lighthouse were abandoned. The air was so still that one was afraid to disturb it. The drizzle of the previous day had evaporated under a warm sun and the horizon was obscured by a grayish haze which seemed to rise like steam and then blend into a soft blue. The glassy swells rolled lazily in and shattered themselves into fragments of flashing silver against the worn rock. Gulls spread their wings and soared proudly above, silhouetted against the deep hue of the sky. Then, coming out of the distant mist, a steamer pushed its way southward—its heavy columns of black smoke suggesting that men were hidden away in dark recesses.

Now that the surroundings were drying, my thoughts turned to fishing. Inside the dwelling, the simple furniture felt cold and clammy and held little attraction, but outside, the surf was comparatively placid for the first time in weeks, and with the minus tides, one could survey parts of the rock hitherto inaccessible. Those seldom visited climbs were below the landing platform around the end of the fissure, where the seas often charged through with unbelievable clout. Here is where I would try angling, hoping for a bonanza. Wouldn't a fat salmon make a nice morsel for dinner? The only available pole was badly battered, and the line twisted. It was a challenge to make it halfway usable.

My experience with the kelp flies prompted me to take the Flit gun along as "standard" fisherman's equipment.

As I climbed over the slimy contour on the seaward side of the fissure, a small indentation appeared, the best parallel to a fisherman's chair—and it was out of the line of vision of my cohorts.

Using sea worms removed from the incrustation, I cast out my feeble line, but whirlpools and currents sucked it back repeatedly. The hook snagged on seagrass, barnacles and mussels, and sometimes the latter snatched the bait. This fruitless effort went on for perhaps an hour. Then I gave up in disgust.

None too anxious to return empty handed, I stretched out to soak up a little sun. The kelp flies were all over me so I put the Flit to work. Finally the warmth so relaxed me that despite the rocky mattress I fell sound asleep. When I awakened sometime later, the sun had vanished and a strong southeast wind was kicking up its heels. Leaping up quickly, I could see the breakers licking at my feet, threatening to inundate the ledge. Hastily I crept across the first barrier, slipping all the way until reaching the end of the fissure, which was flooded with each onrushing wave. Still, it was the only escape route as the south wall was perpendicular.

Fear gripped me. One false step and I could end up in the witches' brew boiling below. Over the second crest I caught a brief glimpse of the lighthouse lantern looming high above, but it was quickly lost in an exploding veil of white spume.

For some reason my absence had not been noticed. I was totally on my own. Watching for the right moment to skirt the end of the fissure demanded a long wait. When I finally got up the nerve, the dash was through an ice-cold shower of drenching salt spray. I slipped and fell and almost rolled off into the ocean, but by wriggling like an eel and using the tips of my bleeding fingers I made it to the other side, a much wiser individual.

George met me at the top of the steps.

"Where yah been?" he growled. "Where can yah hide around this place?"

When I told him, I received a harsh warning which, summed up, came to, "Don't ever try a stupid thing like that again!"

On the very next day word was received by radio that the lighthouse tender *Rose* was on its way with water and fuel for the supply tanks. Though the rain barrels were full, the tanks were low and the drinking water tasted of rust. Toward late afternoon the vessel was sighted cutting her way through the foaming ridges at an eight-knot gait. When she anchored under the shadow of the rock, I noted the brightly painted buoys on her well deck. A busy roster of replacing buoys awaited the *Rose* down the coast, so without the fanfare that usually took place on such occasions, the crew of the visiting ship immediately readied the hoses. As we secured the lines and placed the nozzles in the hungry tanks, the ship's pumps went to work. A northwesterly wind was at the vessel's stern quarter, and despite her anchor, she experienced difficulty holding her position.

To permit the correct flow and protect the hoses, the lines had to be changed constantly. It was as if the tender were giving the rock a blood transfusion. The 395-ton *Rose* was a holdover from the Lighthouse Service years, a rugged vessel that had rendered yeoman service. Once classified as a U.S. Lighthouse tender, under the Coast Guard she was known as a buoy tender and was certainly qualified under either title, having minded thousands of navigation aids in the Pacific Northwest and Alaska since entering service in 1916.

When the excitement of "operation refuel" ended, instead of watching Roy hit his golfball, I got into a conversation with the others on submarines. Being the outer sentinel that we were, our eyes were always open for any such sightings, but inasmuch as the war was winding down, the vigil had slackened.

Captain Tagami, master of the Japanese submarine *I-25*, earlier in the war had shelled Fort Stevens, 15 miles north of the lighthouse. His submersible had also torpedoed allied ships off the shores of Washington and Oregon. Other Japanese submarines had wreaked havoc as well but only sporadic enemy submarine operations were reported off the Pacific coast after 1943. Most of the excitement came from the Fort Stevens incident. On surfacing at night, Tagami had taken a fix on Tillamook Light, which offered him a highly suitable guidepost. During that period, tensions ran high and sharp lookouts were kept at the rock. But while Tillamook Light continued to blaze at full intensity, the other coastal aids to navigation were extinguished. Old Tillamook must have been rather a comfort to the enemy.

Several times the keepers admitted possible sub sightings within the vicinity of the lighthouse, but never did the enemy give any indication of wanting to shell the old sentinel or shatter its brilliant probing beam.

My interest now shifted to a new project. I began looking around the confines for some old bottles in which to place notes. I planned to cast them into the sea and await an answer. The others thought I had flipped, but I had always been fascinated by ocean currents and the way they transport floating objects from one place to another. Naturally, I had visions of the notes reaching the hands of a Polynesian maiden in a far-off exotic land or perhaps the attention of some interesting Oriental. My messages told about Tillamook Rock and environs in glowing terms. My name and address were always attached.

With the first big wind, I tossed the glass containers into the brine, figuring that it would be months, perhaps years, before any would be found. But, lo and behold, that coveted day arrived much sooner than I had expected. In fact, when the motor lifeboat returned to the rock a few weeks later there was among my mail the following letter:

Sir:

My husband is in the fish business. Recently he was called upon to dispose of a dead sea lion that was washed up on the beach near here. The owners of a nearby resort offered to pay him to get rid of the stinking animal, and my husband took the job. While ripping open the sea lion's stomach, he found a bottle which had a burned rag around its top. On

closer search he discovered that said bottle had a note inside. Strange to say, it told of some tripe about Tillamook
Rock being a paradise isle. My husband says you must be
nuts. He fishes out of the Columbia River and often passes
the rock in his fishboat. He says it's the most Godforsaken
place he knows of. As for those handsome men mentioned in
your note, my husband said he once looked at the rock
through his telescope, and the faces at the railing almost
scared him to death. He asked me to answer your letter, as
he is too busy. I just got home from the cannery where I
sling fish, and took a minute out to write this letter.

Yours truly,

Mrs. B——— F———

Needless to say, that was one project in which I quickly lost
interest, and there were no more replies. Perhaps the other bottles
are still afloat somewhere in the world, encrusted with great
growths of barnacles.

One evening after sparring with the slightly deflated punching
bag hanging in the fog signal house, I overheard the head keeper
and Ed arguing over who left the big ring around the bathtub.
Both pleaded innocent but I had scrubbed it out well after my last
bath, and I knew Allik kept everything in apple-pie order, so it
had to be one of the two contestants.

Baths were permitted only once a week because of water and
fuel limitations, and that weekly bath was always a treat. The old
tub, with legs like a bow-legged sow, was a porcelain relic, but it
held lots of water and was long enough and deep enough for one
to get well immersed.

The keepers told me of erstwhile attendants at the light who
hated to take baths and would sometimes go weeks without doing
so, or until growlings from the others drove the dry one to the
wet place.

Despite my early hatred of the rock, I had gradually grown
very fond of it and had learned a whole new side to life, that of
being in a lonely place and yet finding fulfillment in the natural
wonders of God's world. Where else could you be on a small islet

with a perfect 360-degree view of the ocean in all of its varied moods, a place with a grandstand seat for the most beautiful sunrises and sunsets of any place in the world? Where else could you better see the endless string of sea birds flying south in the fall or watch the vast aquarium of mammals and fish cavorting about.

I became hooked on lighthouses, and old Tillamook, despite its scars, was the hallmark. I could relate to one of the erstwhile keepers before my time, a faithful old individual named Bob Gerlof, who would never leave the rock when it came his turn for shore leave. Puffing his old corncob pipe, he had a secret love affair with the place, and when age finally forced his retirement, he religiously went to the seawall at Seaside each evening to be sure the light was burning properly.

Sea conditions were not the best on this day when the lighthouse tender approached the rock. (Smith Scenic Photo)

# CHAPTER 10

# RELEASED

When the motor lifeboat arrived in early October, a letter for me came marked, "Official Business." It contained word that a transfer awaited me on termination of my present vigil. The news struck like electricity, and instead of jumping for joy, my sentimental attachment for the place I had once loathed, surfaced. Never was there a spot that could hold a candle to the peculiarities of the rock, nor of its colorful attendants. Though a slightly dismembered branch of common society, each was diversified, and in a sense, a legend in his own time.

Since my first horrible night on the rock, many chapters had unfolded, and now that my final departure was near I somehow knew I was going to miss the natural surroundings; the untamed, changing seascape and the moods of weather. Above all, I would long for the ocean, a capricious destroyer yet a thing of beauty. Then the rock—an ancient remnant, all that remained of a lava flow which long ago had succumbed to the raging seas.

Sea fever was a disease which I had contracted from living by the ocean, and as if giving me a royal farewell, the Pacific was again at its best with another of its magic tricks. Its entire expanse had turned red, pink and magenta, like a shimmering carpet— one solid mass of wild color which on closer examination proved to be masses of jellyfish, each the size of a dinner plate, and each boasting long, streaming tentacles. As far as the eye could see, brilliant hues obliterated the aqua tint of the ocean. The translucent organisms moved in umbrella-like fashion, expanding and contracting like boiling paint pots. Their tentacles with sharp sting potential could have brought agony to one unfortunate enough to be cast into their midst.

They were in such profusion that their close union had a soothing effect on the ocean, similar to that of heavy oil slicks. For almost three days the red horde remained, their numbers increasing until they overlapped one another. Then, mysteriously, sea birds, thousands of them, swarmed in from every direction to prey on the jellyfish. Predominant among them were the terns and gulls which swooped down like dive-bombers from crazy heights. The sea of jellyfish, as if doomed to extinction, remained at the surface where the birds could peck them to pieces. It was a bountiful feast for the ravenous creatures, and they ate so tenaciously that few were able to take flight. Bloated, they paddled around aimlessly, pecking at more of the delicacies. Soon there began to appear holes in the carpet, revealing the blue of the ocean, and then new flocks flew in from rookeries to engage their gluttonous counterparts in combat for the remaining organisms. Brutal battles ensued and the more the jellyfish were depleted in numbers, the more savage the contention became. Feathers from wounded birds became as numerous on the surface as the jellyfish had once been. Sometimes five to ten birds would fight over a single morsel of transparent substance, but it was usually the newly arrived birds that defeated their fat adversaries in the fierce combats.

Two days later, the last of the red carpet was consumed, and as if waved off by a magic wand, the birds flew away as mysteriously as they had appeared. Again the red sea turned blue-green.

Indian summer brought an ocean serenade to those waters. Whales came close to the rock, shooting geysers skyward. Porpoises danced and chased one another; playful hair seals and sea lions poked their heads from the frigid waters, each enjoying one last fling before winds would again climb the Beaufort scale and sea billows roll violently under the clouds of winter.

Many of the birds were bidding adieu to their northern haunts, winging their way southward, blackening the horizon in unbroken chains. The sea air had a stillness about it and the evening sunsets were a profusion of color.

I could hardly believe it was to be my farewell, nor was I sure of the reason for my transfer unless, perhaps, George could no longer stomach my cooking. He had been off on leave and there had been a more relaxed atmosphere around the rock. Though all of the keepers had uniforms, seldom were they ever worn except for special occasions ashore or when a Coast Guard inspector was due. For the most part the uniforms were like those used under the Lighthouse Service, natty, dark blue with brass buttons. Under that regime orders stated they were to be worn every day. But I learned from the keepers who came up through the transition, that unless the principal keeper was a strict disciplinarian and an adherent to the rules and regulations, dress codes remained relaxed. There was no way an inspector could make a surprise visit to Tillamook Rock. By necessity, he had to make his plans known several days in advance, giving plenty of opportunity to get the station shipshape, the dress uniforms cleaned and buttons polished.

I remember it well, waving farewell several days later, being lifted up in the breeches buoy and peering below for a final bird's-eye view of the seemingly primeval rock, crowned with its watchtower. The 36-foot motor lifeboat, like a drifting Dutch shoe, rolled violently below as the seas came up to meet her. Tough little self-righting cockleshell that it was, one could not help respecting the designer of such an able craft.

Craning my neck in another direction, the wind smarted against my face and the sea spray appeared to be spitting at me spitefully. Looking down once more at the acres of ocean, the rock seemed so small. Against her bosom leaped splendid breakers blowing themselves in a million silver sparkles on impact with the solid mass. Cumulus clouds gathered on the horizon like black sheep waiting to intermingle with their cirrus counterparts overhead.

As the scene unfolded, all seemed quiet over the house of Tillamook. Like tin soldiers, Allik, Ed and Roy, all in the derrick house, waved. Wonderful characters that they were, I was sure our paths would someday cross again. It also entered my mind that, just for oldtimes' sake, I might be accorded a final dunking before reaching the boat. Swinging pendulum fashion, I kept wondering how long it would be before this derrick boom and mast would be swept into the sea like those before.

The boat jockeyed below. Suddenly I felt the cable zoom out as if I were falling through space. My heart came up in my mouth when my fall was finally stopped with a jerk. I looked up at my cohorts in the derrick house; grins masked their faces and I knew this was just a little something to remember them by.

The boat worked itself into position, heaving and rolling, its cutwater sometimes coming clear out of the brine. Pulled aboard by two Coastguardsmen, I scurried aft to the cockpit to feast my eyes on the old crag. That same pungent smell of the sea filled my nostrils as it had on my first arrival. This time, however, it was pleasant to the senses. I also thought of the occasions before when the lifeboat had been delayed for many days because of irascible sea conditions, but this day it had been on time and I was scheduled for the outbound voyage.

And so had gone life in a lighthouse—one day up and the next day down, grousing about everything and nothing—depression, melancholy, contentment, joy, variations of storm, fog, calm. Labor was paid for but with no bonus for the dangers, except perhaps the ever-present coffeepot perking on the kitchen stove. Life in a lighthouse sounds drab and lonesome, you say? Well, maybe, but to me it didn't quite figure out that way. . . .

As the boat gathered steerage way against a beam sea, whipped into lumpy, incongruous shapes, I scanned the rock as though it were the closing scene in an adventure film. Screeching gulls were lined up in ghostly procession on its lower reaches just out of grasp of the watery fangs. Black clouds and the evening haze closed around the lighthouse with profound mystery as if it were an ancient castle rising out of the mist. Soon only the beam of light was visible, shining out to sea as it had for many decades, warning seafarers away from the jaws of destruction.

Soon all the bight lay in a gulf of shadow, leaving only the sheer cliffs inshore standing bare in the dusk. As the lifeboat came closer to the spreading reaches of sand forming the spit, an occasional watery hulk was uncovered by the ebbing tide. Then around the south jetty, across the mountainous swells of the bar, came the glow of the lightship and Cape Disappointment astern. Finally the friendly lights of Astoria.

Tragedy at the entrance to the Columbia River. This 191-foot, $3.25-million tuna seiner, the *Bettie M.*, is shown hard aground after stranding on March 20, 1976. She struck the bar sands and eventually settled near Jetty A. To the right is Cape Disappointment Lighthouse and hovering above is an Air Force helicopter. All eleven men aboard the vessel were rescued by the Coast Guard. The seiner carried 900 tons of frozen tuna. (Seaside Photo by Sam Foster)

# CHAPTER 11

# RETURN TO TILLAMOOK

More than a decade had slipped by since my tenure on the rock. Then one day while working as editor of a Seattle maritime trade weekly, I was thumbing through the local Notice to Mariners when I chanced on a note asking for comments from interested parties regarding the abandonment of Tillamook Light as an economy measure. Once before such an inquiry had been forthcoming from the Coast Guard, but the commercial fishermen had protested vehemently. This time, however, the Coast Guard was more than just asking.

The station was the most expensive lighthouse to operate in the 13th District and one of the most costly in the nation; its equipment was antiquated and in bad need of repair; its location was no longer vital to merchant shipping, which utilized innovative electronic navigation aids including the Columbia River Lightship radio beacon. Furthermore, the service branch indicated that an unmanned, specially designed ocean buoy could be placed a mile west of the rock and adequately do the job for a fraction of the cost of operating the lighthouse. The age of automation was being ushered in and the Coast Guard aids to navigation officer at district headquarters informed me that the day was fast approaching when all lighthouses would be automated.

The protests against the closure of Tillamook were insufficient. The closure date was accordingly set for September 1, 1957.

I wanted to go back just once more. Because I had kept in touch with Ozzie Allik through the years, arrangements were made for me to join members of the press on the buoy tender (Coast Guard cutter) *Mallow* for the trip from Astoria to the rock, just prior to the closure of the station.

It was indeed an epic voyage and hard for me to express the feeling that came over me when I found myself up, up, up, in the breeches buoy and being swung around and lowered to the landing platform. It was one of those very special days. The ocean was flat, an inviting aqua-silver color, and the headland along the shore, a deep purple. The lighthouse hadn't changed, the sun reflecting from its white walls and black lantern house. All appeared in the customary apple-pie order, including the little "Chic Sales" on the side of the precipice. Surveillance by faithful guardians was in evidence.

And a faithful guardian the rock had. That guardian was none other than Oswald Allik, still at the post, rounding out 20 years of service on the rock. No longer an assistant keeper, he had been in charge for several years. The others had retired from service or passed away. George Wheeler had died while fishing on the Columbia River. Roy, in his sunset years, had been awarded the Gallatin Medal for faithful lighthouse service, though he probably would have preferred a new golf club. In place of the old-timers were Robert Sevanson, Jay Peterson, Jim Jordan and Mike O'Donnel, all young Coastguardsmen. Their periods of duty had been altered considerably. Instead of long stretches up to three months at a time, with two weeks off, newcomers were on duty 42 days and off 21.

Peterson, who operated the hoist and creaking derrick, landed me with ease, and a grand reunion it was with friend Allik. The years had been kind to him; he looked almost as I had last seen him.

After a few other members of the press were landed, I could contain myself no longer and made a mad dash up to the light-house to visit all my old haunts. There were stacks of materials being readied for shipment to the base. Even the lighting appara-tus would be removed from the lantern, and after the closure date, never again would a light shine from the tower.

Just as on the day of my first arrival, I inspected every nook and cranny from the fog signal (or engine) room to my secret hideaway, the inner sanctum on the second floor. My bedroom was unchanged, my eyes first falling on the porthole where the wounded goose had entered. In fact, all was as I remembered it. Allik told me the tower ghost still did its haunting act on certain nights.

There was something grand about the music my feet made on the iron grates of the circular staircase. The kitchen stove where the lightning bolt had nearly electrified me was still in use and I noted a slight ring still visible around the bathtub. The old punching bag still hung from the ceiling, half deflated. The same old compressors and generators, the water and fuel tanks and the coal bin were all there. Outside, considerably more scars were evident from the winter storms and violent seas.

Allik confessed that he and his crew had been busy sealing cracks in the floor, walls and ceiling with plastic cement. The structure was creaking in the joints like a tired old man. He told of the recent storms tossing several rocks over the 134-foot-high lantern top, many weighing 20 pounds.

On only a couple of occasions in "Tilly's" history had the light failed to shine and then only when awesome storms spawned seas that sent rocks, green water and sea life into the lantern and lens. But Allik proudly recalled that not once in his 20 years of trustee-ship at Tillamook had the light failed, including the severe storms of 1952.

"The winds were 80 and 90 miles an hour that night," Allik recalled. The waves crashed clear over the light, and rocks smashed through three panes of glass that guard the lens. The supports of the roof over the light were bent and water washed down the circular ladder inside the light into our quarters. But the light never went out, and new panes (a large supply kept on the rock) were installed as soon as the seas subsided."

Tillamook Light's replacement, carried aboard the *Mallow* the day of our visit, was a big red buoy marked *2TR*. It gave its first guttural honk of triumph over its huge white predecessor at 1:30 p.m. after hitting the water one-half nautical mile due west of the rock. It was a considerable effort by the *Mallow's* deck hands, directed by Chief Boatswain's Mate Francis Lewis. They had to wrestle with ten tons of buoy and nine tons of "sinker."

The $23,000 buoy, containing light, radar and fog signal, would almost pay for itself in a single year. During the 1950's, it cost more than $15,000 annually to operate the old beacon. Lt. Mort L. Jackson, skipper of the *Mallow*, had little to say about the transition but performed the task with precision.

Highly honored was I when Keeper Allik asked if I would write for him the last entry in the station log. Trying to catch his thoughts and some of my own, the following was inscribed, an entry that a few weeks later was reprinted on the editorial page of the Portland *Oregonian:*

Farewell, Tillamook Rock Light Station. An era has ended. With this final entry, and not without sentiment, I return thee to the elements. You, one of the most notorious and yet most fascinating of the sea-swept sentinels in the world; long the friend of the tempest-tossed mariner. Through howling gale, thick fog and driving rain your beacon has been a star of hope and your foghorn a voice of encouragement. May the elements of nature be kind to you. For 77 years you have beamed your light across desolate acres of ocean. Keepers have come and gone; men lived and died; but you were faithful to the end. May your sunset years be good years. Your purpose is now only a symbol, but the lives you have saved and the service you have rendered are worthy of the highest respect. A protector of life and property to all, may old-timers, newcomers and travelers along the way pause from the shore in memory of your humanitarian role. September 1, 1957.

It was just a few days after my visit that the light was extinguished, and final preparations made for evacuation of all hands. The station furniture and heaviest equipment, including the generators and compressors, were left in tact. Even the head keeper's desk, the kitchen stove and refrigerator remained. Only the items for which the Coast Guard might have future use were off-loaded. All personnel were removed by the usual fashion until it came to the man operating the derrick. He made a daring leap to a small craft, leaving the rock in solitude for the first time in three-quarters of a century.

Hundreds of sentimental viewers at Seaside and Cannon Beach were greatly saddened the night of September 1, 1957, when for the first time in nearly eight decades the lens in the crown of the lighthouse failed to shine. Blanche DeGood Lofton, Portland poet, expressed it well:

### Tillamook Light 1881-1957

Shorn of her light and her glory,
Abandoned, forsaken. . .bereft;
Deserted by tender and keeper!
The last lone man has left.

Forsaken—but never forgotten,
As we walk the wet sands of the night;
The darkness a presence beside us,
Awaiting the beacon's old light.

Tillamook earned her retirement—
Over three score and ten were her years!
Spare her your grief and your pity—
The valiant have no time for tears.

It is I, the lamenting, the lonely—
The light may be glad for her rest!
I might become reconciled. . .only,
The night is so black in the west!

It was one second past the hour of midnight, September 1, 1957, when Head Keeper Oswald Allik tripped the switch that cut off the light. Some 80,000 candles then gave way to the new buoy's mere 400. The watery acres around the old crag would thereafter be dark by night and the waves would no longer catch the shimmering reflection of the probing beacon.

122      *Tillamook Light*

Publicity on the closure was widespread, reaching even to foreign publications, for the old sentinel had always been a vital part of Oregon, even though separated from the mainland. Oregonians loved the old lighthouse with its awe and mystery. Many memories were rekindled and stories published concerning the rock. Mrs. W.W. Banks, while searching through some old papers, discovered a long-forgotten letter among her possessions. Its contents were published in the *Seaside Signal*, in 1968, telling of early life on the crag. It was written from Tillamook Rock on November 27, 1919, by Howard L. Hansen, first assistant. Hansen's letter, written to Mrs. H.A. Cornell of Ecola, Oregon (Cannon Beach was once called Ecola) follows:

"Received your letter asking for information about our light, so will try and describe it. We are out here on a lone rock about one mile from shore. We have no communication with shore only when one of the tenders brings us provisions and mail—sometimes once a month and sometimes in the winter time we are here 60 to 70 days without a boat.

"The light is about 130 feet above the water. Seas come over this in the winter time with such force as to break the heavy plate glass around the lens, putting out the light and causing considerable work to get wooden shutters in the place where the glass is broken out.

"The lens has twenty-four bulls-eyes that throw out the rays of light, revolving around once every two minutes, causing a flash every five seconds. The light is a vapor light on the same principle as these mantle lamps they pump up with air and heat a little tube so as to generate a kind of gas. After going through the lens this light has developed 48,000 candle power. The light is lighted at sundown and runs until sunrise.

"The buildings are built of stone and brick. The main building is made of stone blocks a foot square and three feet long, each block being fastened to the others with copper bars so as to stand the pounding of the sea. The tower rises from the center of the building. There are eight rooms beside the tower. These are our quarters, kitchen, storeroom and office.

Coast Guard cutter (buoy tender) *Mallow* stands off Tillamook Rock in 1957. The vessel brought the new buoy TR2, which replaced the lighthouse as an active aid to navigation.

Void of human life, the old sentinel stands alone in disgrace. (E.A. Delanty photo)

"The siren room is built onto the west end of the main building. There are two eighteen-horse-power semi-diesel engines that run the compressors which pump air into a big tank. This tank, when running the fog siren, is kept at 40 pounds pressure. A valve is opened at regular times by the engine to let the compressed air rush into the siren. The siren is composed of two brass cylinders, one revolving inside of the other, caused by the air rushing through them. This siren is run whenever it is so foggy that we cannot see five miles.

"In landing on the rock we have a derrick that we swing out with a steam donkey and lower a cage down to the lifeboat from the tenders. Our provisions or men get into this cage and are hoisted up. Sometimes when the cage is lowered down they miss the boat, with the result that whoever happens to be in it gets wet.

"There are five men allowed to this station, four men on the rock with one man on shore on his vacation. At this time there are five of us on the rock. The keeper is a man 61 years of age, the other four are from 18 to 23. One of the young spent 10 months in France with the army, so we have some very interesting stories after work.

"We spend the forenoons cleaning up around the station, keeping everything in the very best of shape, and to help pass the time away. The afternoons we have to ourselves to read or pass the time as we please. In the wintertime it gets rather lonesome as we have to keep the windows all closed tight and cannot get outside of the house very often. You have very likely heard stories of men going crazy out here and also that there is a big iron band around the rock to hold it together. These stories are all made up by somebody who had so much spare time that he did not know what else to do.

"We all are glad to know that there is somebody who can watch our light and listen to our fog siren and who takes enough interest in us to write asking for information. Although we may not be able to get over to the beach to see our nearest neighbors, by next summer we will have a telephone cable between here and there. Some 25 years ago there was a cable from here to shore but it did not last long. It broke and was never replaced.

"You asked why it was a revolving light instead of stationary. The main reason is that a stationary light is very often mistaken for some other light and sometimes is the cause of a wreck."

Less than two years after closure (1959), Tillamook Rock was put in the hands of the General Services Administration for displacement. After the state of Oregon had refused possession, the rock and its lighthouse were placed on the auction block. The publicity was widespread, the interest intense. Here was a piece of real estate offered, where one could have his own private island with all the amenities built in. There was a warning that accessibility was extremely hazardous, but it failed to impede the interest of scores of bidders. It seemed as though everybody wanted to own a piece of the rock. The writer confesses he talked his publication into making a ridiculous bid of $100, being fully familiar with the problems. Nobody else who had ever been connected in any way with the rock or its operation offered a bid.

Of the other numerous bidders from all over the nation, none had set foot on the rock and most had never seen it. Still others didn't even know where it was located. Some 400 persons responded to the GSA advertising in the summer of 1959, 60 of whom placed solid bids. The sealed bids were opened in Seattle, and Academics Economic Coordinators of Las Vegas was the high bidder at $5,600.

Who were the Academic Economic Coordinators, people wanted to know. For what devious reason would such an unlikely Nevada organization want an abandoned lighthouse?

Their original offer of $4,000 had been raised twice by wire before the deadline. They evidently wanted it badly. Right behind them was Marcel Delotto of Garden Grove, California, at $5,002. The other bids ranged from a low of $2 to $3,170, most of the bidders thinking they would be purchasing the ideal island retreat.

Rumors spread like wildfire. AEC was believed by the uninformed to be a front for the Mafia. Others said big-time gambling would be started off Oregon's coast. When it was learned that AEC was a bona fide firm, having interests in research, contracting and investment, rumor persisted that the rock would be used as a secret research area for nuclear bomb components.

Despite some attempted landings on Tillamook Rock, from a fishboat on calm days (during which only a couple of representatives managed an hour or two on the rock) it remained virtually uninhabited for the next decade. The sea birds reclaimed it as a rookery, and seals and sea lions clambered up on the lower reaches at the east end. Kelp flies flourished. Storms blew out their lungs on the place and waves continued their dastardly work, gradually but surely taking their toll.

Sam Foster, longtime resident of Seaside, photographer, news, and T.V. man, and perhaps the biggest local booster of Tillamook Rock, got together a plan for revisiting the lighthouse more than a decade after its abandonment. He had first to get AEC's permission and then talk Allik—who had rounded out his government service days as the last keeper at Heceta Head Light—into joining the expedition. The historic trip of August, 1969, is best told in Foster's own words:

"With its mighty beacon no longer flashing warnings seaward, Tillamook Rock Lighthouse presented a portrait of desolation as a group of men, including the last lighthouse keeper, Oswald Allik, paid it a nostalgic visit one day last week after a 45-minute dory ride from Cannon Beach. The lighthouse shows the toll of 12 years of neglect during which coastal elements have buffeted the structure since its closure in 1957, after 77 years of continual operation.

"The lighthouse and its rock are owned by a group of Nevada investors and permission was required for the visit. The party including Allik, Bruce Luzader, a Portland photographer with his son Bryant, and the writer, (Sam Foster), made the four-hour trip. Partners in a commercial dory fishing venture in Cannon Beach, Mel Ohlson and Larry Pershin, offered to take the group out, and Seaside resident, Murl Kilndt, provided back-up boat service. Both boats were launched just south of Haystack Rock in Cannon Beach. Wind and weather were ideal.

Above: The engine room, or fog signal room, housed the generators and compressors, batteries, electrical systems and tools. Buda, Sullivan and Hercules engines provided the power. The coal bin was also located in the area. Below: Junkman's bonanza, the lighthouse fog signal and engine room. The fog signals had not blasted for many years. At center right can be seen the old punching bag retired like a punch-drunk boxer. (Seaside Photo by Sam Foster)

"The eastern exposure of the lighthouse, facing the coast, is the natural access, since all other sides are sheer. The original plan of mounting the rock was to tie the boats together, put a wet-suit swimmer into the water with a line that could be secured on land, and pass the camera gear hand over hand to the rock. The method was tried but the boats banged together so hard they had to be separated frequently. An alternate method, waiting for lulls in the cresting swells and rushing at high speed to the edge of the rock, was devised. A mistake in timing could have meant swamping a boat or a man by the wall of water.

"Safely on the rock, the party started up the long stairway to the building. The stairs were more than half-filled by the accumulation of bird droppings. The double doors of the north entrance had not been opened for more than 10 years, when two of the Nevada owners secured the place. The first room inside the doors was the generator room, the largest room in the structure. The interior lay masked in darkness. The odor of mildew and dampness filled the air.

"Generators and a long bank of storage batteries filled the end of the room. At the slightest touch, layers of flaking rust fell off the power plants which had once served mariners so dutifully. 'They were left behind when we left and are certainly no good now,' explained Allik. Stepping over fallen pieces of plaster, he led the group by flashlight through the main level.

"The kitchen, now bare except for cabinets and an old refrigerator, gave no evidence of the fragrant aromas that once came from there. In other rooms were sagging bed frames which once cradled weary keepers. Calendars showed September, 1957, as the last month of usage. All drawers in the wooden furniture were warped beyond use. Allik's room of long ago showed the same disrepair.

"The second story, the work and storage area, was even more damp than the main floor. Floor boards felt spongy to the wary walker. The tower, where the powerful lamp and lens were once housed, is reached by iron wedge steps that spiral upward from a center shaft. The huge expanse of glass provides the same breathtaking view of the oceanscape enjoyed by mariners and keepers since it was built in the 1880's.

"After two hours on the rock, ocean winds were becoming stronger and a quick exit was in order.

" 'The inside is about gone, but the outside, with those three-feet-thick walls of Clackamas stone, should last a long time,' reflected Allik, casting a last look at the sleeping sentinel on the rock."

For Allik it had been like walking into a tomb, and one can imagine his sadness at seeing the deplorable condition of the old sentinel. The owners, AEC, which had been organized with five individuals—according to Frank Rogers, one of the owners—grew to 51 members after the lighthouse acquisition. The hat was usually passed to pay the lighthouse taxes. The assessor had never dared to board the rock to estimate its value, basing taxes solely on the sale price. Those taxes rose from $104.66 in 1966 to $127.62 in 1969, according to Clatsop County records.

Ancient lighthouses never die. They just fade away like the proverbial old soldier, and certainly Tillamook was tottering on the brink.

# CHAPTER 12

# THE NEW OWNERS

For the man who has everything, we don't recommend a deserted lighthouse.

Why would a highly successful, New York General Electric engineer want to buy a lighthouse? And of all lighthouses, why Tillamook Rock? It all happened in 1973, when George Hupman, senior executive with General Electric (in Philadelphia) involved an Oregon real estate firm in negotiating a deal with AEC of Nevada. Negotiations were firmed for an $11,000 cash purchase.

Hupman's friends said "he was nuts," his wife accused him of having "lost his marbles," and those familiar with the dilapidated guano-deep white elephant claimed he had purchased $11,000 worth of fertilizer. But George Hupman was a man of determination and vision—in this case, mostly the latter. He claimed his new island kingdom to be "Magnificent! Simply magnificent!" And, if anybody could do anything with the place, he had both the ingenuity and the money. He further would not have to worry about landings by boat because he could hire helicopters at Astoria or Seaside when conditions permitted. It could be a retreat well away from the proverbial noise and pressure, thought he.

With connections the world over, Hupman claimed some of his Japanese friends had even promised to come over to teach the rock's cormorants to dive for fish. His initial visit by copter was in July of 1973.

Two others who flew in through the fog to the lighthouse described it as a "real dilapidated mess." They suggested that if

130

Innovation for the rock. Something that the lighthouse keepers never knew was helicopter transportation from the shore. Here, a small pontoon whirly bird, piloted by Gerald Casman, is used to bring visitors to the rock in July 1978.

George Hupman, former owner of the rock, and wife Jeanne, with Robin Chapman and Roger Thompson, KGW-TV8, Portland. Hupman purchased the rock from Academic Economics Coordinators of Nevada in 1973. He paid $11,000 for his "castle" and sold it five years later for $27,000. (Seaside Photo by Sam Foster)

Scenes of the destruction at the lighthouse as seen by Oswald Allik, Sam Foster and others on the return to the abandoned station in 1969. Closed 12 years earlier, it had been totally neglected. (Oswald Allik photo)

Deplorable was the only way to describe the interior of the lighthouse after being abandoned for more than a decade. The light's former keeper, Ozzie Allik, displays a chagrined expression while sitting in his old desk chair. (Seaside Photo by Sam Foster)

someone offered Hupman a keg of ale and a $5 bill, he would sell it on the spot.

"No way would I sell it," said the excited GE official, after prowling through the damp and rusted buildings for about an hour. "It is in better shape than I expected it to be after being abandoned for 16 years. The buildings need sandblasting inside and out, and then they can be made very livable for a vacation hideaway." Hupman estimated it would take thousands of dollars to equip the buildings for casual living.

The 53-year-old man made a "college try" at attempting to rectify some of the storm damage and to clean up the mess on the interior, but the effort was tantamount to a fly attacking an elephant. He brought an eager crew to the rock by copter, and from time to time got others to come out and help. A good path was made through the bird droppings on the outside and in cleaning up the fallen plaster on the inside. The press played up his activities to the hilt. Was there hope for the dying sentinel?

Hupman, who years earlier had spent some time in the Northwest directing construction on Oregon-California power projects faced his new challenge with enthusiasm.

His initial work crew included Al Kottke, a GE employee relations executive from Schenectady, N.Y., who replaced a broken window pane in the lamp room; Rudy Koehler, a GE scientist also from Schenectady, who checked out the electrical system, along with Lew Ford, a Portlander who works for GE in New York City; D.T. Galarneau, GE field engineer in Portland, who tended to carpentry chores, and Mrs. Hupman and Ford's wife, Mary, who sloshed from room to room with mop and pail.

Things were beginning to look somewhat rosier. In fact, Mrs. Hupman even planted a seedling fir tree in an obscure exterior corner, claiming that maybe her husband "hadn't really lost all of his marbles after all." She and her friend were probably the first women who ever slept overnight at the lighthouse.

All the while, Hupman extolled the future of his new castaway, trying to overlook what he really down-deep knew was an almost impossible task. He even went so far as to have a little gas-powered generator (for lights) flown out. The owner figured it would take about $10,000 to meet the immediate needs of the lighthouse. Among other things he wanted a "cocktail lounge of sorts" where the lens once revolved.

Skeptics shook their heads, but always-optimistic George kept thinking big. Occasional brief visits were made till the summer of 1975.

"There's a complex set of reasons behind it all," Hupman insisted. "It offers something interesting and something I'd like to do. It's a part of Oregon and the West Coast—which we've come to love since we lived there. No matter how much you may like a place like Oregon, unless you've got something like this, you just never quite get around to coming back."

But Hupman did get around to not coming back. The winters came with their furious results, the little seedling fir tree withered and died; the rookery got into full swing again, cormorants, murres and gulls whitening the rock as if a snow had fallen. The repairs the Hupmans made were eradicated. More cracks opened and more weather broke through. A copter from a logging firm made an unauthorized landing and its occupants messed up the place. A tower storm door was left ajar and several cormorants came inside to nest. Sea water flowed through.

On April 23, 1975, Osward Allik, still a legend in his own time, died from a heart attack after trying to rescue the driver of a wrecked car on the Salmon River road near Lincoln City. At 73, Allik, a native of Tallinn, Estonia, had spent 32 years in the Lighthouse Service (20 years on the rock) and the Coast Guard, ending a highly colorful career. He was the last survivor of the rock's civil service keepers. Well-attended rites with military honors were held in Portland, his wife Alice insisting that he be buried in service uniform, with a book which this writer had previously dedicated to him, placed at his side.

Since closing Tillamook Lighthouse in 1957, and keeping Heceta Head Light until its automation in 1963, Oswald Allik had been enjoying retirement in Portland. He had epitomized the ideal lighthouse keeper, and his death was almost simultaneous with the end of an era when virtually all aids to navigation became automated, losing once and for all the personal touch.

The author's nomination for the photo of the decade. This aerial shot of the light-house shows the takeover by hundreds of cormorants and murres which turned the rock into a rookery after the human element departed. This is the way the place looked in the sharp camera eye of Sam Foster in the mid-1970s. From count-less eggs popped scores of fuzzy little fur balls. Some unwanted visitor of the human sort had left the rear door of the lighthouse open and several of the feath-ered friends had taken up lodging on the inside. Their calling cards were highly odoriferous. The rock had become strictly for the birds.

Proud new owner of the rock. Max M. Shillock Jr. of Portland gets his first closeup look at the disheveled lighthouse sitting atop the rock, smeared with bird droppings. (Seaside Photo by Sam Foster)

The last of the derrick—the boom, the mast and its supports were carried into the sea in the fall of 1978. The owner of the rock, Max Shillock, filed a loss claim with his insurance company but payment was refused. (Aerial photo by Sam Foster)

Tillamook Rock Lighthouse was abandoned to wind and wave until 1978, its erstwhile master having lost interest in his islet castle, claiming as the reason, "pressing business demands elsewhere." In January of that year, Hupman sold out to 25-year-old bachelor Max M. Shillock, Jr., of Portland, who had never set foot on the rock but purchased the guano-encrusted "dream house" for $27,000 cash. A professed investor, he conceded that it would not be inaccurate to "call him wealthy." A dedicated collector of Coca Cola memorabilia, his interest had spread to retired lighthouses. He had seen the rock as a child, and later as a college student touring the coast had decided he'd like to own it.

His initiation in June was somewhat unusual, for he was to get his first close-up view through eyes blurred by seasickness. Arrangements had been made with Cannon Beach skipper Bob Hart to take Shillock out to circle the rock in his 23-foot dory. Hart, assistant Darrel Moore and two newsmen awaited Shillock's arrival in his silver Lincoln. When the young purchaser eyed the craft and the breakers, he was openly apprehensive about boarding, dressed as he was in tie and corduroy sports jacket—rather dressy apparel for the adventure. Still, his curiosity about the rock got the best of him and the trip got underway from just south of Haystack Rock. Unaccustomed as he was to boating, the 90-minute cruise in near 80-degree weather was not to his liking, the rolling ocean causing a feeling that kept him in the bow where he could either view or heave—whichever desire came first.

"I'll tell you what you bought," Moore said with a laugh as the boat neared the rock, "one of the largest natural supplies of fertilizer in the world." Moore was referring to the bird droppings left behind by the hundreds of seagulls, cormorants and murres that made the bastion their home. Hart guided his boat in a circular course around the lighthouse as Shillock began a visual survey between bouts with *mal de mer*. He groaned on seeing that one of the large windows in the tower had been broken, wondering if the birds that covered the rock were nesting inside the lantern.

This apparent storm damage led the new owner later to insure his treasure for $25,000, including fire, vandalism and liability. The first close-up view didn't delight him, but he vowed to return soon. He was true to his word, but the next attempt nearly cost him his life. On July 8, he and three others made an attempt to reach the rock in a small outboard motorboat. The craft overturned in the breakers near Seaside, all of its occupants being thrown into the surf. One, a James Sealy, was drowned. His brother Dan, Gerald Major and Shillock—all suffering from hypothermia and shock—were discovered by a Coast Guard helicopter as they struggled toward the beach.

Shillock then decided if he was to set foot on his new acquisition it would have to be by helicopter, and that's the way he finally got there. Like his predecessor, he had grand ideas for the sentinel. He enjoyed the resulting publicity and announced he wouldn't resell his lighthouse for less than $1 million. In fact, he reputedly listed it for $750,000 with a Los Angeles real estate firm.

While Shillock's plans unfold, the winter seas continue their assault and the lighthouse slowly succumbs. The lantern supports grow weaker and new cracks appear. Already the rock has gone through three private owners, and probably in the wings waits another and still another. Undoubtedly Mother Nature will win in the end, for without an unlimited bank account and a steady watchman to see to old Tilly's needs, she is doomed. Still, the stone walls put together so well by the great Ballantyne may last for a long, long while.

Perhaps it would have been best, after the light was extinguished, if the state had accepted the old monument, made it off limits forever to trespassers, and designated it as a wildlife reserve "strictly for the birds."

# APPENDIX I

*Observations of the eminent George Davidson, U.S. Coast and Geodetic Survey, author of the Pacific Coast Pilot, between 1882-1889, concerning Tillamook Rock and its lighthouse.*

The sea-coast light is one of the most important upon the northern coast because it marks the approach to the Columbia River. The lighthouse is built upon Tillamook Rock, 175 yards in extent and (formerly) 115 feet high, with a subordinate summit to the south-southeast. It is a bold, basaltic mass lying one and one-fifth miles south 41 degrees west (S. 41° W.) from Pinnacle Rock at the western extremity of Tillamook Head. As it rises from the ocean, the face of the rock on the west side is precipitous for 15 feet, then breaks back with an irregular slope for a short distance, and then rising to 80 feet, it leans over to seaward. The large, rounded knob above this has been blasted away to make a flat surface for the buildings about 90 feet above the sea. The north side is nearly vertical. The east side slopes gradually to the sea under an angle of one-fifth. There is a deep fissure on the south side separating the secondary summit.

The water on the west, north and east sides of the rock is from 25 to 40 fathoms deep, but shoals to 16 and 18 fathoms on the south side over a limited area. The sides of the rock are so steep that it is reported by the lighthouse keepers that whales are frequently seen rubbing their barnacles off against the rock. Before operations were commenced here, the rock was the resort of thousands of sea-lions.

The light is a primary seacoast light of the first order of the system of Fresnel. The structure consists of a stone building about 46 feet square, and 18 feet high to the top of the slightly sloping roof. The building faces east with a large door and two windows six feet above the roof of this building to the iron balustrade, above which brick walls are carried eight feet farther to the base of the lantern. Each side of the tower has one window.

Above the tower is a lantern with a round dome. There is a one-story fog signal building, about 30 feet square, of the same height as the main building, attached to the west side thereof. All these structures are painted white, except the lantern and dome which are painted black. On the east side, on a lower level, is a small brick building containing the hoisting engine, and a derrick for handling supplies.

The light was first exhibited, January 21, 1881. It shows from sunset to sunrise a flashing white light every five seconds. The length of the flash is about 2½ seconds, and of the dark interval 2½ seconds.

When passing close to the rock in October 1885, we timed the light as follows: The very bright flash 1½ seconds; the total eclipse 3 seconds; but there was a secondary brightness of half a second's duration preceding the brilliant flash. This secondary brightness could not be seen when several miles distant. The light is seen around the entire horizon; but its range of visibility upon safe water is between the bearings southeast by south, half south (SE. by S ½ S.) round by the south and west to north by west one quarter west (N. by W. ¼ W.)

The base of the building is 88 feet above the mean level of the sea, and the height of the focal plane is 136 feet above the mean level of the sea. Under favorable conditions of the atmosphere, the light should be seen from a height of—

> 10 feet at a distance of 16.9 miles
> 20 feet at a distance of 18.4 miles
> 30 feet at a distance of 19.6 miles
> 60 feet at a distance of 22.2 miles

When this light was established, the flashing red light at Point Adams (lighthouse) was changed to a fixed red light. (Point Adams bears north 16 degrees, 15½ miles from Tillamook Rock.)

During southeast storms, the great swell of the Pacific from the southwest rolls with tremendous force upon this rocky islet, and owing to the open gorge on that side, the waters are driven over with great fury; large pieces of rock have been cast upon the roof of the dwelling, 115 feet above the sea. It is reported that in the great storm of 1882 the waves were swept over the top of the lighthouse.

When Tillamook Rock Lighthouse was being built, part of the stones (cut rock) for the building were carried off the rock in heavy storms. Some of the barrels were found cast ashore as far northward as the Quenuialt River (Quinalt River), a distance of 85 miles, perhaps due in part to the Davidson Inshore Eddy Current.

The fog signal at Tillamook Rock Light is a first-class steam siren which gives blasts of five seconds' duration at intervals of one and a half minutes, in thick and foggy weather.

The number of hours during which the fog signal is sounded per month exhibits the relative amount of foggy weather. In general, the months of August and September have the longest periods of fog. The following are the number of hours for each month during 1886: January, 24 hours; February, 26 hours, March, 39½ hours; April, 3⅔ hours; May, 9¾ hours; June, 13 hours; July, 14½ hours; August, 133¾ hours; September, 94 hours; October, 40¼ hours; November, 21¾ hours; December, 43 hours.

It is to be remembered, however, that there is probably less fog at Tillamook Rock than at the entrance to the Columbia River, as the following extract from the journal of the superintendant of construction of the lighthouse (Tillamook), under date of March 1880, will show:

> It has been observed since coming here in October (1879) that there has not been a dense fog on the rock, and that it is generally clear to westward when there is a dense fog hanging over Tillamook Head and the Columbia Bar, or that when the mainland cannot be descried at all, it is generally clear for several miles to the westward.

There is a rock awash inside Tillamook Rock and one-third the distance from the light to the nearest part of Tillamook Head. It is about 30 yards in extent and bears north 67 degrees east (N. 67° E.), distant 740 yards from the light. Although there is a depth of 15 fathoms of water near each rock and between them, and also between the danger (halfway rock) and the head (Tillamook Head), yet no strangers should attempt the passage except in a great emergency, because the currents are strong and variable.

Vessels bound for the Columbia River from the southward can safely pass within less than a mile outside the lighthouse in 30 fathoms of water. . . .The coast should not be approached nearer than on a course to the rock (Tillamook) of north by west one-quarter west (N. by W. ¼ W.). After passing the rock, a vessel should not pass to the eastward of the line joining it with Cape Disappointment Lighthouse. A course northwest by north (NW. by N.) from the rock will lead to the Whistling Buoy off the Columbia River bar (1887), distant 13½ miles.

*Tillamook Rock Buoy*—This is a 60-foot spar buoy, painted white, lying in 23 fathoms of water 250 yards northwest by north from the lighthouse on Tillamook Rock. It is used as a mooring buoy for the lighthouse tender when supplying the station.

*Hydrography off Tillamook Rock*—One mile off the light-house, the depth of water is 33 fathoms over a bottom of fine dark-gray sand; 40 fathoms at two miles over similar bottom; forty-five fathoms at four miles, similar bottom; 55 fathoms at eight miles with both green mud and sand; and at ten miles, 61 fathoms, similar bottom.

*Regarding Tillamook Head*—On some old maps this head is erroneously called Cape Lookout. Upon one we find it called Cape Mezari, and upon another Cape Misaria. DeMofras calls it the Cap N.S. de la Luz. The U.S. Exploring Expedition of 1841 calls it Killamuke Head. Tebenkoff very faintly copies Vancouver and has no name. The Coast Survey reconnaissance chart of 1850 calls it Killamuck Head. In 1851, when we were occupying Cape Disappointment, it was known as Tillamook Head and that name has continued.

(Tillamook Rock's name derivation followed that of the great headland, inasmuch as it was considered nothing more than an obstruction to navigation until it was crowned by a lighthouse. The Indian name Tillamook (or Killamuck) means "land of many waters." Author's note.)

# APPENDIX II

*Federal political climate during the tenure of duty of
Tillamook Rock Light Station 1881-1957.*

Just before the erection of Tillamook Rock Light Station,
several changes in federal government administration were
taking place. An act of Congress on August 14, 1875 provided
for the prosecution of persons who "willfully and unlawfully
damage any property or vessels of the Lighthouse Service, punish-
able by a fine not to exceed $1,000." Masters of lighthouse tenders
were given police powers in matters pertaining to government
property and smuggling by an Act of Congress, June 16, 1880,
and duties of Collectors of Customs relating to lighthouses were
transferred to the Lighthouse Board.

In 1882, the Secretary of the Navy began a vigorous cam-
paign to transfer the Lighthouse and Lifesaving Services, plus
the Coast Survey, to the Navy Department. His efforts, however,
met with such stiff opposition from the Secretary of the Treasury
and others that he gave up the fight.

In 1884, uniforms for male lighthouse keepers, masters, mates
and engineers of tenders were first introduced to "aid in main-
taining its (Lighthouse Service) discipline, increase its efficiency,
raise its tone and add to its esprit de corps." The following year,
all 1,600 men in the service were outfitted with both dress and
fatigue uniforms by mandatory order.

On July 26, 1886, Congress passed the Reorganization Act
dividing the country into districts. (Tillamook Rock station was
in the 13th District.)

During the administraion of President Andrew Jackson, a
policy that had an adverse effect on all government services was
adopted, that of playing political football for federal appoint-
ments. The "Spoils System" fouled the Lighthouse Establishment throughout its early history, perhaps reaching its most
flagrant abuse under the Grant administration. In the case of
the Lighthouse Establishment, the Collectors of Customs Appointed lighthouse and lightship keepers with impunity, not

always according to ability but according to which political party one favored.

The Spoils System peaked on July 2, 1881, when Charles J. Guiteau, a mentally unbalanced individual, unsuccessful in his bid for consulship in Vienna, assassinated President James A. Garfield. The tragedy shocked the American people into demanding reform. Thus, on January 16, 1883, (two years after Tillamook Light was established) Congress passed the Pendleton Civil Service Act. President Chester A. Arthur, himself an ex-collector of customs, was given authority. The situation slowly improved, and in 1896, President Grover Cleveland brought the U.S. Lighthouse Service wholly under the Civil Service Act.

On July 1, 1903, the Department of Commerce and Labor was created by the Congress to facilitate the expanding economy and trade of the United States. The Lighthouse Board, Coast & Geodetic Survey and other agencies concerned with navigation were transferred to the new department. During the next seven years, the Lighthouse Board, under which the service had operated since 1852, came under severe criticism for its mode of operation by Department of Commerce secretaries, Oscar S. Straus and Charles Nagel, who insisted the Lighthouse Board could no long administer control over the growing magnitude of responsibilities. Resulting friction created a division of authority in each district between the Naval inspectors and the Army engineers.

On June 17, 1910, Congress dissolved the Lighthouse Board and created the Bureau of Lighthouses in its place. The changeover called for a Commissioner of Lighthouses, a chief construction engineer, and a superintendent of naval construction to be appointed by the President of the United States.

On July 1, 1910, President Taft named highly capable George R. Putnam as commissioner and Arthur V. Conover as deputy commissioner. Under Putnam the service found stability. He remained in the post for 25 years.

In 1938, following the great depression, President Franklin Roosevelt ordered the U.S. Coast Guard and the Lighthouse Service to study how they could be combined, as an economy